THE BIG ISSUE PRESENTS

Letter to My Younger Self

INSPIRATIONAL WOMEN

Devised and Edited by
Jane Graham

BLINK
bringing you closer

First published in the UK by Blink Publishing
An imprint of Bonnier Books UK
4th Floor, Victoria House, Bloomsbury Square, London, WC1B 4DA
Owned by Bonnier Books
Sveavägen 56, Stockholm, Sweden

Hardback – 978-1-788706-45-2
Ebook – 978-1-788706-46-9

A CIP catalogue of this book is available from the British Library.

Designed by Envy Design Ltd
Printed and bound by Clays Ltd, Elcograf S.p.A

1 3 5 7 9 10 8 6 4 2

Blink Publishing is an imprint of Bonnier Books UK
www.bonnierbooks.co.uk

*Dedicated to all the people who have ever
sold or bought* The Big Issue

Contents

Chapter 3: Self-belief

Chapter 4: Inspiration

Chapter 5: Independence

Chapter 6: Family

Chapter 7: Friendship

Chapter 8: Motherhood

Chapter 9: Self-image

Chapter 10: Rebellion

Chapter 11: Transformation

Chapter 12: Ageing

Chapter 13: Hindsight

Chapter 14: Love

Foreword

The first volume of *Letter to My Younger Self* was published in 2019. After 12 years of the weekly feature running in *The Big Issue*, during which time it had developed from a single column I pitched to the Scottish edition to one of the most popular and talked about double-page features in the UK magazine, it felt like a good time to take stock. We had hundreds of uniquely intimate interviews with some of the most intriguing, talented and powerful high-achievers in the world. We knew there would be a public appetite to read (or re-read!) some of our most insightful encounters, to get inside the heads of daredevils, megastars, rebels and trailblazers like Ranulph Fiennes, Paul McCartney, Werner Herzog and Margaret Atwood.

Over the years the weekly 'Letter to My Younger Self, has garnered a reputation for discovering new truths about interesting people. Big stars are unusually willing to reveal personal information in their interviews, perhaps because *The Big Issue* is trusted as a magazine with integrity, unlikely to seek out big headline controversies or exploit sensitive material.

That first volume did not entirely stem the feeling that a lot of terrific material remained unearthed. A second volume was inevitable. What struck me going over the multitudes of great interviews – including many conducted after the release of that first book – was the emergence of particular threads among women; experiences, frustrations, aspirations and regrets shared by women of all ages and backgrounds. The content of Volume Two became obvious. Because what a collection of female voices can do, that even the most enlightening of books by individuals can't, is draw out those themes – career ambitions, relationship worries, psychological barriers, disappointments and rewards – which connect numerous women regardless of class, race or other differences.

As I read over the selection in this book I became fascinated by these similarities. An early lack of self-esteem was notably common, even in some of the most ostensibly outgoing and confident characters. Despite decades of success in films and TV shows, actor Alison Steadman said she still 'worried that I was about to be found out for being rubbish'. The much-celebrated Baroness Shirley Williams MP, regarded as a political powerhouse, berated herself for having what she called 'a deep female tendency' to aim for the second top job, and wished she'd had the nerve to run as Leader of the Labour Party. Dawn French recalled how her confidence went up and down, and admitted how jealous she felt when her comedy partner Jennifer Saunders had a huge hit without her.

We might remember her as a formidable presence in folk music and civil rights campaigning but Joan Baez described her young self as 'angst-ridden, extremely shy and fearful'. Even the effortlessly glamorous Debbie Harry of Blondie said the main impact of media interest in her was to make her feel awkward, unsure of how her male colleagues felt about her being in the spotlight.

Anxiety about appearance, and how others might judge one in relation to it, also ran high. She began her career as a model but actor Keeley Hawes described her young self as a 'gawky, gangly' girl who 'always thought there were other people better than me in the room'. James Bond star Rosamund Pike said she 'was not the one boys were interested in' and remembers anxiously covering her 'embarrassingly rosy cheeks with corrective green make-up'.

Gavin & Stacey writer and actor Ruth Jones and soul singer Mica Paris were among many who recounted how their weight affected their confidence, either in regard to self-perceptions or professional pressures. After having her first child, Mica (at size 14!) was told by her record company she looked 'like two people in one body' and would have to go into training. When she was just a size 12, Ruth said she spent a lot of time just thinking about her weight, the issue constantly 'playing on my mind'.

TV stalwart Joan Bakewell, fabulous firecracker actor Anna Chancellor and the formidable Jess Phillips MP spoke movingly about their regrets regarding marriages entered too early or pregnancies which, in hindsight, perhaps came along too soon. There are a number of memorable stories in this book about broken marriages, heartbreaking abortions and young women struggling to be confident mothers when they were still unsure what kind of adults they were turning into themselves. Such concerns were voiced by far fewer of the men I've interviewed – more common among those were regrets about not being around enough when their children were very young.

Another thing I noticed was how complicated many women

felt their relationships with their mothers were, though most managed to form better friendships as they got older. As for dads, presenter Mariella Frostrup, who 'hero-worshipped' a father who 'wasn't that interested in children' was just one of many who adored their fathers but felt they had to work hard for the attention they craved. Actor Honor Blackman remembered her fear of her father, who sometimes 'whacked' her, and slapped her face when she first put on make-up, but she loved him just the same. The uniquely frank Eileen Atkins, star of numerous popular TV shows and movies, had a family life full of the most incredible experiences; her jaw-dropping revelations led to one of the most talked about interviews *The Big Issue* has ever run.

You will notice in a number of interviews there are pauses, ellipses and unfinished sentences. Here, I have tried to convey moments when the interviewee has been caught by the emotional impact of pulling up a half-buried memory or considering someone important in a new way. Conversations about lost connections, periods of great happiness or sorrow, or unsatisfactory endings to relationships often led to unexpected waves of affection for undervalued parents, loyal friends, life-changing teachers or, perhaps most pertinently of all, their own innocent young selves, before they knew what life was about to throw at them.

Despite the varied struggles and obstacles experienced by many of the women included here, I very much hope that this book will leave you full of optimism and inspiration. I have tried to put the chapters in an order which reflects the trajectory of a fulfilled woman; from her early dreams, through transformations and trials, towards a mature understanding of what is truly important in life. Every story is one of ultimate

Foreword

success and achievement, often against what looked like insurmountable odds. So many times I've finished an interview and, upon walking out of the door or clicking 'leave' on the Zoom meeting, wanted to punch the air, buoyant and in awe of the awesome woman of substance and strength I've had the privilege of spending time with. When I finally hold the first finished copy of this book, I know who I'll pass it straight on to. It will go to my teenage daughter. Who could be better?

Jane Graham
Books Editor, *The Big Issue*
May 2022

Lord John Bird

Co-founder of *The Big Issue*

The 'Letter to My Younger Self' interviews remain one of *The Big Issue*'s most popular, and long-running, sections. They are unusually insightful and often uplifting. It is appropriate and right that volume two of the interviews focuses on the truth of women's lives. For a long time, these have been the voices and experiences that were ignored, not taken seriously, or filtered through male lenses. I am glad we have got here.

My mother , Eileen Mary Dunne, had a good hand because she had gone to the nuns for schooling until she was 16. Then it was the farmyard and the house and the fields until she was 18 when she said, 'sod this for a game of soldiers' and went off to London. Her elder sister was already there with a husband and a young child. The Irish were unwelcome in many parts and she ended up in what were then the slums of Notting Hill. But her good hand at writing was not to be called upon. The only job on offer was that of a barmaid in a pub on the Portobello Road. On her night off she met a piano-playing labourer in another pub and she was married soon after. She stayed in London, had six boys and lived mostly a life of torment.

Torment for being Irish, torment because there was never enough money to be got from her husband's wage packet. Torment because he could be a drunken and violent man. Eviction followed eviction and soon her boys were in the care of a convent for displaced children. And then a council flat in a block of social housing in Fulham, away from Notting Hill. And then another torment: I started to get in trouble at school, with the police and even the park keepers at our local park. 'You'll kill me,' she would say as we sat in juvenile courts or police stations, or she visited me in institutions for young offenders.

Decades of misery led in the end to her death at 52, always a cleaner in later years, and bringing up her children. She smoked like a chimney, and drank copious cups of thick tea with sugar, and ate poor food, so it was no surprise that she left us so young.

Aged 18 and fresh out of a young offender institution, I stopped my father from pouring a kettle of hot water over my mother and I burst the bullying days asunder. Another finger laid on my mother would lead to the bully being bullied.

Violence towards women hurt me more than anything about growing up poor. About growing up ignorant of our responsibilities for each other. My mother was the making of me. Cantankerous, rude, outrageous in some of her opinions, but the woman who made me a human being, in more ways than one.

Letter to My Younger Self: Inspirational Women

I wish the world would recognise that living in a male world is not a true world. It is a lopsided, upside-down world that does not put women and their incredible abilities, skills and insights central to that world. That righting that misbalance is like the fight for climate and social justice, the road which we need to take. My mother first made me realise how misguided this world was, and how we needed to sort it soon.

Chapter 1:

Ambition

Emily Maitlis

Journalist and broadcaster
8 January 2012

I was a big girly swot at 16. I enjoyed school and theatre and drama. I thought that was where my future would lie. Until I asked my mum if she thought I could be an actress and there was a slightly too long pause. And I thought, oh, I think she's just told me I'm not very good.

I think your position in the family is really key to how your personality develops. I was quite a bit younger than my sisters and as a result I had a more relaxed upbringing than them. My eldest sister made things easy for me, she was quite rebellious and stretched all the boundaries for me. I was very lucky. My parents gave me a lot of freedom and were very trusting of me. I remember they went away when I was 18 and said I was free to have a party in the house. That was very trusting of them. It was a very good time actually. Both of my elder sisters had left home and my parents relaxed quite a lot. I remember my mum, when I was about seven, saying she knew what was going to happen; I would hit 14 and get frightful and difficult. She made me sign a little note promising not to get too uppity when I got to 14. I remember signing and thinking, she's been through this before. Now as a mother I try not to want something too hard for my children, so that they don't rebel against it.

I really want to stroke the arm of my teenage self and tell her to stop worrying. I really thought when I graduated that it would be the end of my intellectual life, no one would ever ask my opinion on anything again. I panicked about exams, about my weight, about never achieving anything. I imagined working in a factory screwing lids on toothpaste tubes. I'm much happier now than I was at 16.

I don't think I was a very ambitious teenager but I was impatient. I graduated from Cambridge at a time when the UK was very unappealing, around the '92 recession. And I thought, God this is grim, I can't fill in another form and get to the back of yet another queue. I got a job in Hong Kong and my real coming of age was there. It was incredibly liberating. People handed you their business cards and told you to call them on Monday, and you did and they were expecting you. It was a punchy, exciting place to be. People took a chance on you – you could be cheeky and forward and it would pay off. The UK seemed very correct and proper and sluggish in comparison. I spent nearly a decade there before I got a job with Sky News in London.

I'd tell my younger self to stick at it and not be so terrified. When I first started in news, I was terrible. I still had an arts mind. I was sent off to interview Chris Patten (former Hong Kong governor) when he was opening some shopping centre in China, and my report would start 'the shopping centre is 60ft high and made of some of the finest glass and steel...' and they were like, no, no, what did he say about human rights abuse in China? And I'm thinking, oh, I didn't ask him that. I dreaded reading the papers because I'd see a story I'd been on and all the Chinese journalists had taken the story much further. I was certain I would never ever catch up. It was very hard.

The most unpleasant thing for me was doing breakfast at Sky. All my Friday and Saturday nights were ghastly – they started at 6pm and ended at 9am. I had a whole year of that and it made me really low. Everyone has their Achilles heel and that was mine. It drove me mad. I really admire the people who do it brilliantly. I was completely confused the whole time. I was exhausted and unhappy and I never got to grips with that.

If I could go back and tell my younger self about my life now, she'd say, you lucky bitch, what a fluke. But I'm still very superstitious – I always think, God it could all collapse any day. I'm constantly reminding myself how lucky I've been so far, wondering when will it all go wrong. I had the most brilliant education but it was a state education and I was never given the confidence public school seems to give people, to believe they can be prime minister, rule the world. Without the Hong Kong experience I don't think I'd have had the chutzpah to go for the jobs I did.

If I could go back and relive one moment it would be when I was on a train in Italy and I had a phone call from my parents, telling me my place at Cambridge had been confirmed. It was a proper hand of God moment. I know that makes me sound such a girly swot but you know what, I am. This Italian soldier started chatting me up and he asked for my address and I said, it's Queens' College, Cambridge. And I thought yes! I've done it.

Baroness Warsi

Member of the House of Lords
17 February 2015

Of all the five sisters, I was probably the dad's girl. And the one who wanted to know what was out there, in the wider world. Whenever there was a family get-together and the women were all chatting in one corner and the men in another, you'd find me with the men. I was never very interested in a certain kind of women's conversation. I found them quite fickle. Two of my closest friends when I was a teenager were men. The roles between men and women are completely blurred now but when I was growing up there were male roles and female roles and I wasn't interested in what I felt instinctively were female roles. Clothes, hair, make-up they never meant anything to me. I just wasn't interested. My elder sister liked all that, she loved to go shopping, but I hated it. My mum bought all my clothes and I'd be happy to wear whatever she chose. My main interest was books, I always had my head in a book.

I was very aware as a teenager that I was lucky to have such a good education as a Muslim girl. Not everyone around me had the same, and I felt I had a responsibility to make the most of that. My mum always told me and my sisters, we had to be better than the boys. I was very conscious of that. We were always encouraged to have an opinion.

My mum says I was a really easy teenager. I never gave her any hassle – I saved all that up for later, as she puts it. I wasn't moody, I didn't want to be out with my mates, I wasn't going partying, I wasn't wearing make-up. I didn't have a lot of friends, but that was an active choice because I wasn't particularly interested in the things they were talking about. I was really interested in bigger issues – identity, what it meant to be black and British. How I fitted in. I remember learning about the British Raj at school and constantly questioning how my teacher presented it, the creation of Pakistan, that kind of thing.

In terms of a career, that was very much chosen by my mum when we were teenagers. She decided she needed a lawyer, an accountant, a teacher and a pharmacist, and she just told us which one she wanted us to be. I got law. So I became a lawyer.

When I was a student, I became very involved in student politics. I was definitely on the left. I came from a strong Labour family. I remember fighting for grants, not loans. And against the poll tax. When I got into my twenties I started thinking more about domestic politics and it became pretty obvious the things I believed in made me centre right. Low tax economy, smaller state, civil liberties, opportunity, all of that. I didn't actually join any party until my late twenties because I felt the issues far outweighed party politics. But I think if you want to be involved in frontline politics it has to be done through a party.

One thing I'd say to the young Sayeeda is to learn to have more fun. It's not instinctive for me to just go out and have fun. The job's always more important to me, and I would always choose work over play. I think I'm a workaholic. But I'd tell my younger self to learn to play more.

My kids say, I don't know why you complain about Nana because you're turning more and more into her every day. Yes, I'm probably quite focused, like she was, but less driven as far as my kids are concerned. I tell them their options and the consequences that flow from them, but they have to make their own decisions. If one of them wanted to run off and join the circus? I'd tell them the advantages and disadvantages and if they can live with the consequences, so be it. People don't always take responsibility for their actions. I tell my kids they must always do that.

If I really wanted to shock the younger me I'd tell her she ended up married to a man she knew and despised at high school. I got married and divorced before that but I've ended up with this man who was in my year at school, and we'd hated each other. We rubbed each other up the wrong way. My kids like to think it's because we had a crush on each other but that's completely untrue. We finally got together after I'd travelled the world and he had too.

I would probably tell my younger self to hold back more. At times I was far too blunt and honest and open. I was naive. I didn't understand the politics, the game-playing, of politics. I probably still don't. I remember one occasion, in a private meeting in Parliament, and I was quite upset by something and showed a lot of emotion. I shouldn't have done it. I was far too transparent. I refuse to say all decisions should be made only with your head. But they can't all be made with your heart either. I think with women it's probably more heart than head. But if I had to choose between a politician who felt too much and one who didn't feel at all, I'd always go for the one who felt too much.

The young Sayeeda in her wildest dreams wouldn't have thought she'd end up at the Cabinet table. She might have expected to play some part in politics, most probably as a lawyer, maybe as a campaigner. But not a Cabinet minister. That would not have been a world she felt entitled to enter. The idea of being able to walk into the Palace of Westminster and say, yes, this is where I work. Even when I first got there, I felt like I was waiting for someone to walk in and tap me on the shoulder and say, what are you doing here? And then, being part of the Tory Party – chairman of the Tory Party! That would shock the young me.

If I could go back to any time in my life it would be when my daughter was between nought and five. They're so clever and cute at that age, always learning. At that time I was running my own business, my own legal practice, working incredibly long hours. I have some great memories of that time but I wish I could relive all of it all over again with her. Just without the bad marriage.

Shirley Williams

Former Member of the House of Lords
20 February 2010

At 16, I was already interested in politics. I used to run about carrying poll cards for the Labour Party when I was a girl. I knew I'd go into politics one way or another. I was determined to leave school and get into the world, so I never went into the sixth form at all. As soon as I got into university I pushed off out of there. I worked for about a year on a farm, then in a hotel, because I wanted to see the different ways people lived their lives out in the country. I cycled from London to Newcastle to see what the experience was like. I was very interested in the emergence of post-war Europe after the Second World War so I spent some time in Germany when I was 16, trying to rebuild the German Social Democratic Party.

I was very angry about class, I hated and resented it. I've thought a lot about where that resentment over class came from. I think it came from spending three years in America, in Minnesota, which I was evacuated to when I was about nine. It was such a different city, completely classless – no one had different accents, they all went to the local school. You couldn't tell where someone came from or where they were educated when they opened their mouth the way you could in England. The divisions in England were so deep and I could never understand why. The day I got back to England I remember getting out of my train and hearing the porters and the passengers getting out of first class and noticing that they spoke almost an entirely different language – either cockney or those refined BBC accents. I felt very strongly that that was an unhealthy way to run a society.

If I met the 16-year-old Shirley now I'd probably find her a pain in the neck. I was quite naughty, always causing trouble in school, nearly expelled. I was completely scruffy. I'd quite like the part of her that was very enthusiastic and involved in life and travel and politics. But I'd find her ungracious, a bit hard to take. I don't think many of my teachers liked me.

I'd advise the young Shirley that, sadly, appearance matters more than she thinks it does. And it's going to matter more as she gets older and television is everywhere. I really thought very little about my fingernails or how to attract boys or anything like that. I find the obsession with appearance very depressing now.

I wish I'd had more confidence in myself during my career. I'd tell my younger self that the men I thought of as great post-war heroes of politics, like Attlee (Clement Attlee served as prime minister of the UK from 1945 to 1951) were just flawed men who did some great things. If I'd had more confidence I might have run for leadership of the Labour Party, or the leadership of the Social Democrat Party, which I never did, even though I was the first SDP MP. I suppose I had a deep female tendency to go for the second job rather than the first.

When I took my peerage I made a promise never to use the title. A fat lot of good that did me. I always tell the BBC or any other organisation, just call me Shirley Williams, but there's something deep in the English spirit which makes people very reluctant to drop the 'Baroness', as if it gives their event extra pomp. David Dimbleby, to be fair, doesn't use it, but most people do. I took the peerage to push and publicise the SDP in its early days and in that sense, it was worth it.

Joan Baez

Singer-songwriter

12 February 2014

I have a lot of influences and a combination of roots. My mom was actually born in Edinburgh, and I loved the city when I went there, especially St John's Church on Princes Street, where I found out my grandfather used to preach. When I was 16, I had just learned to play the guitar and it was already a passion. We moved around a lot when I was little so having to always get to know new kids in new schools was a challenge. I found that my route to people, the population of the school, was to be able to sing. I would sing at lunchtimes and they would listen.

I saw Pete Seeger (the American singer and social activist) play when I was 13. I'm still trying to adjust to the fact that he died. Until then I was only singing rhythm and blues, black music with four chords. The white music around seemed provincial and silly. Then my auntie took me to a Pete Seeger concert and the coming together of social awareness, of courage, of songwriting – that changed everything forever.

I was quite an angst-ridden teenager and extremely shy and fearful. For many years I got terrible stage fright. Then I'd walk out on stage and I was another person. As a 16-year-old girl I spent a lot of time chasing around these two people, this driven performer and this shy, anxious thing. They didn't mesh but they were both little old me. But when I sang about what I believed in, my feelings about social injustice, that made me stronger. I was still shy but I was putting forth and that made me stable. I felt I had an idea what I was there for and that made me happy.

Looking back, I think I was a little obnoxious. I never felt I was a dreamer, I thought I was a realist. I was obsessed, I had to say what I had to say. And that got me in trouble. Some people would shy away. Other people thought I was right. And I was right about a lot of things. But sometimes people just didn't want to hear what I was saying. I think I got a hard edge from studying non-violence under Ira Sandperl (an anti-war activist and educator). He had a very hard edge. I learned so much from him. Maybe if my main teacher had been less hard edge I would have done the things I did differently. But I would still have done them.

I had a very poor self-image as a teenager, and that went on into my twenties. It might have come from the fact that during many of my developing years I lived in a town in California which was close to the border with Mexico. Mexicans were not respected. It was assumed because of my name that I was Mexican – which I am, half of me. So I was not treated well. I was overlooked. Mexican kids – well, no one paid any attention to them. Living in that society, feeling there was a prejudice against me, I think I was overwhelmed by it. And now I think that's why I began siding with the underdog. Because I felt like one myself.

Over time my feelings about some of the trappings of fame have changed. From the start I had an aversion to anything commercial. They said I was an impossible diva because I insisted on a black stage with one light and a microphone. I think that actually came out of fear, what would be involved with lots of public exposure. Then, when I had my feet under me, it just didn't appeal to me. If I stayed in an overly expensive hotel because somebody put me there I felt uncomfortable. It was a number of years before I was able to think, you know, the red carpet is there, there's nothing I can do about it, so I might as well get a decent hotel and try to enjoy luxury when it's given to me. Now when I'm travelling it's positively a spiritual experience to live briefly in a hotel place that's beautifully done. And I love it.

I think I would laugh if I read back some of my early interviews. I started proselytising when I was 17! And I was so certain. I would argue with anybody. I went on right-wing radio stations because I knew I could have a good heave-ho. I remember one presenter, testing my non-violence beliefs, asked me what I'd do if someone attacked me on the subway. I said maybe I'd throw up. And apparently the backstage crew were cheering, yeah, get him! I could spout off these answers. I hope I've become more forgiving and less strident as I've got older. But I still think I gave some pretty good answers when I was young.

When I was with Bob (Dylan), we were very young. We were very involved in doing the music and hearing the music but we were also aware that this phenomenon was going on around us. I think mostly it was fun at first. Going to England with Bob in the sixties (captured in the 1965 documentary *Don't Look Back*), it was complete chaos. One of the keys to it was I didn't do drugs. So I was totally outside the circle of crazy-making people and I felt very shut out. And it was getting to the unhappy part of our relationship, blah blah... I don't like harping on that. It all got mended. And what I'm left with now is those songs.

I stayed away from party politics until I endorsed Obama. The sharp 16-year-old me would say, 'Ha ha, I told you so, you can't trust anyone in the White House'. I was moved by Obama's speeches, I thought he was like Martin Luther King. And I'm happy to have felt that wonderful feeling of community we hadn't had for 40 years. I think if he had stayed outside of office and led a movement, we could have made a lot of changes. But that didn't happen. I'm surprised he strayed so far from the dream. He had a photo of Gandhi in his office. I don't understand the man.

I think the younger me would be amazed by the size of the response I've had. Any kid would be shocked at the idea of suddenly becoming a superstar. I wouldn't have a clue what it even meant. It started with me singing a song onstage in Newport (Folk Festival) and bang! That was it. There were 13,000 people there, the most people I've ever seen anywhere. I walked off the stage into *Time* magazine and the rest, as they say, is history. But if you had told me when I was 16 what was going to happen, I'd have said goody.

Baroness Karren Brady

Business executive
11 July 2012

I think I had something about me when I was 16. I was always thinking of ideas and schemes, always pushing the boundaries, always asking why I wasn't allowed to do things. I thought a lot about getting out of my convent boarding school in the middle of nowhere and getting a life. At boarding school, nothing is your own. Your bed's not your own, your hangers aren't your own, you have to book a timeslot to have a bath. I was desperate for independence – and I worked out quite quickly that that would mean I needed my own finances.

My friends would probably have described me then as ambitious. I was always looking for a new idea, another challenge. I was quite a confident teenager. I've never been a slim person but I don't remember there being such an emphasis on how much you weighed in the eighties. What I remember is big perms, big shoulders. I had a big perm myself – I think my hair's still recovering at 42. I had the full gear, the white cowboy boots, ra ra skirts, pixie boots, the whole thing. I see my teenage self every time I look at my daughter. And my advice to her all the time is, you're young – you think this is your life. But it's not. Life really starts when you get a career. That's when you get choices. And the better educated you are, the more choices you get.

My young self wouldn't believe how big football would become in her life – she's the least sporty person you've ever met. Football was a business decision for me. When I was 18 I got onto the Saatchi & Saatchi graduate scheme. Then I got interested in the subject of brand-building around football, about making the crest stand for something. In 1993 that wasn't something that was thought about much. So I thought it was an interesting industry from that point of view. Now I'm interested in all aspects of what goes on in the industry, it's an industry I love. It's what we all do on a Saturday.

I'm not sure how the younger me would feel about becoming a high-profile person. A bit unsure probably, which is still how I feel whenever I see myself on the television. Trust me, there's nothing more scary that hitting your forties and seeing your own face on a 50-inch high-definition TV. But I don't consider myself a TV personality. I'm on TV because of work I do related to my business but I don't do anything else I'm offered – dancing, skating, jungling. I think once you go on TV you have to keep asking yourself, what do you stand for? You have to be very clear about it, or at least I do.

When I found out I had a brain aneurysm, I tried to break

it down into stages. One was discovering I had it. Two was accepting I had to do something about it. Three was choosing what I was going to do. Four was having the operation. And five was closing the door and not thinking about it ever again. Otherwise you spend the rest of your life looking over your shoulder. My surgeon said to me, now get on with the rest of your life, and that's the advice I took.

If I could go back I'd like to talk to both my grandmothers. They were both a big influence in my life, particularly my mother's mother. She was probably one of the feistiest people I knew, always pushing me to the front of the queue, always saying, go on, you can do it, you show them. She died about four years ago and I don't think she ever realised the enormity of the impact she had on my life.

Chapter 2:

Creativity

Ruth Jones

Actor and writer
23 November 2011

I was quite a happy, B-grade 16-year-old, just getting into my drama at school. Home life was fine, with my three siblings. The main bone of contention I remember was my brother Mark's love for heavy metal. I'd be doing my homework and he'd be playing albums called things like Cat Scratch Fever, and I'd be like oh God, it can't get any worse than that. I was into New Romantics myself.

I did think about my weight a lot then. I always thought I was overweight but when I look at pictures now, I wasn't. I was a size 12, a normal figure, but I think my friends were mainly a size smaller than me and in terms of confidence that really played on my mind. I feel very strongly about this issue now, especially with regards to teenage girls. Their weight is such a huge part of their self-image, and they starve themselves. It really frightens me.

I'd tell my teenage self to spend more time with her

grandmothers while they're alive. I really wish I had. Time goes by so quickly, and we just aren't aware of older people who still feel young too, and perhaps feel a bit abandoned by the rest of us.

I remember when *Grease* came out, John Travolta just hit me. I was literally depressed that I wasn't Olivia Newton-John. It was a genuine worry; how was I ever going to look like her? All the blossoming feelings that come with puberty – mine were all aimed at John Travolta. And he had no idea. I did have boyfriends but I think I also enjoyed my broken hearts and unrequited crushes. I still can't listen to The Commodores' 'Still'. It reminds me of that awful teenage wallowing I did.

I think I'd like the 16-year-old me. She was a good laugh and quite a kind girl. But her lack of confidence would annoy me. I'd tell her, you really just do only have one go at this, stop faffing around and go for it. I just thought success was something that happened to other people. I had this idea of not getting too big for my boots, as if there was something wrong with being ambitious.

I remember when *Gavin & Stacey* was given the green light. I texted James (co-creator and co-star James Corden). He'd just arrived in New Zealand, where he was touring with Alan Bennett's *The History Boys* and he said he stepped onto the tarmac and turned his phone on and there was this text saying, 'O, Smithy. We've got the green light.' So that was a nice shared moment for both of us. It was so important for us that that show had heart. There was a lot people could identify with in those characters and there was a lot of love between those families and those friendships in their very ordinary world.

The teenage Ruth would be amazed if you told her she'd be on television one day. She was in awe of that world. She'd just assume the whole fame thing would be amazing. The 45-year-old me would be telling her, yes, but you're only as good as the work you do. It's not about the red carpet or celebrity parties, it's about hard graft. She might be shocked at how much work and how long hours the adult me does.

Judy Collins

Singer-songwriter

20 May 2020

At 16, I was already an old soul. I was desperate about my music – always learning, listening, practising classical piano for two hours a day. One day when I was almost 16, I turned on the radio and this guy was playing folk music. I just flipped out over these songs and I called my father and said, 'I have to have a guitar.' And from then on it was 'The Gypsy Rover' and 'Barbara Allen' instead of Beethoven. And I was going on my father's radio show (her father Charles Thomas Collins was a singer and radio DJ) and going up to the mountains to the Folklore Centre meetings and listening to people singing Woody Guthrie and Pete Seeger songs. It was a very exciting time.

Oh boy, I was a very productive, active teenager. I was the eldest of five. I had to help my mother with the chores and I had to babysit to earn the money to buy all these folk records from the local store; the Clancy Brothers, Ewan

MacColl, Peggy Seeger, all these old Irish and Scottish folk songs. My two best friends were dancers and so we developed a performance of 'The Gypsy Rover' which we played all over town – at the Rotary Club and Lowry Air Force Base and Fitzsimmons General Hospital. We were going to take this thing to Vegas!

I think I'd like the 16-year-old Judy if I met her now. She was very bright. She was a bit of a flirt. She was very intense. She hated her nose – she put a clothes peg on it when she went to sleep. She talked a lot and she was always practising or having to do something. I'd like to have her as a niece or granddaughter or something. She was always interested in everything. But she had also tried to kill herself when she was 14. I would like to say to her, everything is gonna be great. In spite of the fact that you were born with alcoholism in your genetic makeup – my father was an alcoholic, everybody we knew drank – your discipline will keep you from destroying your career before it happens. In spite of your depression, and the fact you're always worried about your weight, and about food, in spite of the fact that you drink, everything's going to work out fine.

By the time I was 19, I was in Boulder, Colorado, I had my little son Clark, my husband was getting his degree and I was working for pennies at the university administration office. I called my father and he got me an audition at a club called Michael's Pub. It was a college hang-out, so it was jam-packed, smoke-filled every Friday and Saturday night. Well, I was shaking in my boots. I dressed like the gypsy rover; I was wearing a pixie outfit with tights and boots and a little silk red top. My hair was very short – my husband had put a bowl on my head and cut my hair. I was very nervous but you know, once I opened my mouth... I mean, I've been performing since I was five years old. I started to feel great. And after I was finished, Mike Besessi, who owned the club, came up to me and said, 'Oh my God.' I said, 'What's the problem?' He said, 'Well, you were great.' And I said, 'Is that a problem?' And he said, 'Yeah, I'm probably gonna have to hire you.'

Do I think 19 was too young to be married with a baby? I don't think I had a choice. There was no way that I was going to make a plan that I could write down and then do. That's not the way life is. I trusted my impulses. And I was very, very disciplined. From the age of five I had to practise every day, do my homework, do my chores. A lot was expected of me. That's the way we were brought up. My father was blind, and he did everything himself. And he wanted us to succeed and to have great grades, and to show up and be stellar performers in our communities. I think that all that time growing up, that's what prepared me for this 60-year career.

I started out listening to other singers and learning songs. My first two albums were traditional songs. Then I moved to New York City and started listening to Pete Seeger, Woody Guthrie and Bob Dylan. I didn't write songs until after I met Leonard Cohen. And he said, 'Why aren't you writing your own songs?' I was the only person in the New York folk community who did not write her own songs. When I started it was slow. I wrote maybe three or four songs a year. Now I'm writing songs every week.

The first song that I wrote after Leonard asked me that question was 'Since You've Asked'. And of course, it became very well known. People know it, they sing it at their weddings. What amazes me is that I didn't ever even think of writing a song before then. I mean, it never crossed my mind. I was always trying to write good short stories at school and I wrote journals, but it never occurred to me. I was raised listening to other people's songs. And my piano teacher was a person who thought if you weren't Mozart you just shouldn't even try. Now I look back at the songs that I've written – songs that Peggy Lee and Nina Simone sang – and it's very hard for me to believe I was able to do that.

Leonard (Cohen) was the real deal. Oh boy. We had a mutual friend in New York – she went to school with him in Montreal – and she would talk about him over dinner. This would be around 1964. She'd say, Leonard is wonderful, we love him. But he's never going anywhere because he writes these poems and they're so obscure and nobody understands them. And then she called me one day and she said, 'Lenny wants to come and see you and play you his songs.' I said, 'Are they obscure?' And she said, 'Yes, they are.' I said, 'Oh well, send him over anyway.' So he came over and he was very good-looking. So I thought, well, I don't care if his songs are obscure – though I never did get involved with him romantically, thank you God. And so he said, 'I can't play the guitar and I can't sing and I don't know if these are really songs.' And then he sang me 'Suzanne' and 'The Stranger Song' and 'Dress Rehearsal Rag'. And I said, 'Leonard, these are songs, and I'm going to record them tomorrow, so just don't worry anymore.'

In 1968 I was in LA and I had just met Stephen Stills (Collins was in a relationship with the singer-songwriter best known as a member of Crosby, Stills and Nash). My album was actually being mixed when this motorcyclist came roaring up to the door at the studio and threw this little tape down on my producer's desk and said, 'You have to record this', Sandy

Denny's new song 'Who Knows Where the Time Goes?'. Then he ran out the door. So we put it on and listened to it, and said, 'Oh my God – of course we've got to record that.' That's what we've been waiting for. It's an amazing song. I love it so much. And I got to know her and I loved her too.

If I could have one last conversation with anyone it would be my son (Clark Taylor, her only child, took his own life when he was 33). He was the best. He was so funny and he always laughed at the things I laughed at. He was the best, the brightest, the funniest, the smartest, the most attractive, and had more friends than anybody and helped many, many, many, many, many people get sober. He was sober about seven years before his death. Now I have his daughter who looks like him and laughs like him and her little boy looks exactly like him too. I would say to him, there are other solutions. Even though I'm a suicide attempter and I know that these thoughts come out. I don't think I talked to him enough about my suicide attempt, but he had that in his DNA. His father's father had killed himself in the same way. But in the end we write our own fairy tales about our lives. And I think that was in his fairy tale.

Cressida Cowell

Author
4 June 2018

I was an earnest, booky little 16-year-old, reading Chaucer and Shakespeare for fun. Jilly Cooper too though! I wasn't at all cool, I was too enthusiastic. I'm still like that. But I was strong-minded and opinionated. I was at an all-girls school which was very academic and didn't take art seriously. They said I was too academic to do art A level, so I left that school and went to one which did take art seriously. I met Lauren Child (creator of the children's book series *Charlie & Lola*), my best friend, there. I was often in trouble at school, I was very dreamy and disorganised and usually late. Teachers don't realise that if you're disorganised, you spend the whole day being told off. It's not very nice.

I had a very split childhood. Most of it was spent in central London, where my dad worked. But he was also an environmentalist, chairman of The Royal Society for the Protection of Birds, and we spent as much time as possible on an uninhabited island on the Outer Hebrides. And there were lots of stories about Viking tribes – the Viking influence is very strong on those islands on the west coast of Scotland. That obviously had an impact on me; I'm still writing about it now. I think I came to enjoy London more as I got older, but as a kid I found it pretty constricting. We didn't have a garden in our Chelsea home, and not many parks. It wasn't a very friendly neighbourhood.

I always felt I could never measure up to my dad (Viscount Michael Blakenham, chairman of the *Financial Times* and the RSPB among other organisations). He was a very strong character. He was a God-like person to me. I'd have to turn into the Incredible Hulk to be that big, that successful, never afraid of anything. I came from a whole family of over-achievers, business people, politicians and suffragettes. What could I ever do to impress that huge, over-the-top family? I think during my twenties my dad was a bit disappointed. I was a clever kid but I wasn't making a mark. He would gently ask, when are you going to get a job?

My first book was published when I was 30 but my first five books were picture books, not particularly 'Wow, this is the next thing'. And *How to Train Your Dragon* wasn't an instant big hit. I think eventually though my parents were very proud, and that was lovely. It didn't change the balance of power between us though. My dad was number one.

My dad's heart was in walking and the countryside and wildness. He was dauntless, not scared of anything. He wouldn't get GPS because it spoiled the wilderness experience. There's a bit in my latest book when you go walking with a giant and he knows every tree, and the story behind every hill. My dad was like that. He made every walk magical.

I admired him terrifically but wasn't a bit like him. He enjoyed being by himself, he was a bit of an island. I'm a very chatty person who wears her heart on her sleeve. He was of the generation that found it difficult to talk about himself and didn't do small talk. He believed in that 'you have to be a man'. We loved each other but there was a big generation gap.

The teenage me would have been so excited by the idea that I would one day have my books published. Authors were my heroes. Ursula Le Guin, Diana Wynne Jones, Tolkien, Douglas Adams. I would have been over the moon at the idea that I'd be on bookshelves near them. Because when teachers tell you, as they often did, that you'll never make anything of yourself, they do get to you. I didn't have the confidence that I would be able to do it. I'd like to tell my 16-year-old self, and my 25-year-old self in fact, not to worry that all her friends seem to be getting their lives and careers sorted, and she's still at art college. I'd say, hang in there! I knew I wanted to write and draw, but it's disheartening to see everyone getting ahead and you're still trying to hang on to your dream. I got my first book contract when I got pregnant, at 30. Suddenly I had a lot to prove, and not at the ideal moment. I've always done everything back to front!

Being a mother does weave itself into your books. *How to Train Your Dragon* could have been *How to Train Your Baby* really. But as well as working out what kind of parent I wanted to be, it was about working out my own childhood. So the book is topped and tailed by the voice of the older, wiser Hiccup, looking back and realising things he didn't see at the time. I was like little Hiccup, trying to live up to this person, his dad, who he loves very much but isn't at all like.

My daughter told me recently her favourite subjects at

school were PE and maths. Suddenly she seemed very far away. I think as a parent you want your children to be like you so you can be close to them. So I was writing with both perspectives. And I also like the idea that parents reading it to their children are reminded of their own childhood of magic and dragons, and can share that with their kids.

As it happens, my dad died very recently. He had a quick, out-of-the-blue illness. He'd just come back from the Galapagos – this is so like Papa – and he was diagnosed with a big sarcoma. He hung on for a couple of months in hospital but he couldn't... The thing is, I didn't think he was going to die. I thought he was invulnerable. I thought he was being surprisingly unlike himself because he did think he was going to die. So we didn't have a big talk. He wouldn't have done that anyway, he was a very private person. Perhaps having his daughter put him in a book (Stoic, the father in *How to Train Your Dragon*) was very hard for him. But I think in the end he was very proud of being Stoic.

If I could go back and live any time in my life again, I'd go back to watching the children playing in the park on a sunny day. They'd be about five and two years old. I loved that. They're so incredibly imaginative, children. We used to go to this paddling pool in the park and they took their little Playmobil figures and spent hours making up little stories together. Then they'd spend hours wandering in and out of puddles, always in the moment. Watching them and being reminded of being a child myself – I loved that. And I miss it so much.

Cornelia Parker

Visual artist

3 April 2017

Sixteen was a tough time for me. My mum had just been diagnosed with schizophrenia so things at home were very unstable. I knew I wanted to do something with art. I'd just spent a week in London with my art class and for the first time in my life I was exposed to museums like the Institute of Contemporary Arts and the Tate. I was a rural, Cheshire child who never went to museums. So that was extraordinary for me, realising what a big world there was out there. My school wasn't keen on students going to art school, they were very academia-focused. I was the first pupil to go to art school.

I was a very shy 16-year-old. I'm not shy any more, but at 16, I hadn't blossomed. I was quite a moody, angsty teenager, introspective. A quiet rebel. I was wearing lots of dark make-up and crepe dresses, lots of second-hand stuff and Biba – I was really into that Biba moment in the early seventies. And

I got into David Bowie and saw him on his Ziggy Stardust tour in '72. For me, he was the best. I was a bit of a loner at school, I didn't see friends in the evenings. I think I was already in art school mode, quite individualistic. My mum complained that I always wanted to be different, but I thought yeah, I do. I feel different.

My father was a very articulate, funny man though he was just a peasant farmer. He also had a dark side. He verbally dominated the house so I don't think I came out of my shell until I'd been away from home for a few years. And then I probably did channel my father, who was this garrulous, flamboyant, rebellious character. I was always the surrogate son among the three sisters, helping him out in our smallholding. My father was very much into my mum but she became mentally ill so she was not available. She was German and had been a nurse in the war. I think she was quite traumatised and became an introvert. She was a good person, I think; my father was more Machiavellian and a bully really. He could swing on a sixpence. He was charismatic, but he could be quite vicious, suddenly, with us. You had to watch out, on alert. I think it made all three of us anti-authoritarian. For me being self-employed was always the only way to go. I didn't want a boss.

Neither of my parents wanted me to be an artist. They'd have been much more comfortable with a proper job, like a doctor. Even when I had some real success they couldn't quite get it. But I think anything I'd chosen, there would have been some issues with it. They did come to see some of my work. When I was nominated for the Turner Prize, I invited them to London and put them up in a nice hotel. My father just spent his time standing in front of my exhibit, 'Church Struck by

Lightning', asking people what they thought of it. I think he was trying to provoke a reaction.

If I could go back in time I'd record my parents, I'd film them. My dad could be hilarious, though he could also be terrible. I think my creativity came from him. But I can see something of my mother there too. She was an interior person, and much of my work is small and interior. The other side of my work like 'The Exploding Shed' is big and explosive, perhaps dealing with the anger or violence that came from my father. I'm always trying to repair something, or bring things back tougher or resurrect things physically, by suspension, so they're not lost. Trying to find something new that comes after the carnage. I think the same thing is happening in the world – as the living memory of the war disappears, people who don't know what that was like seem to get restless, they want to push things till they break again.

Much of my work is about finding potential and salvaging things and I think – I hope – I'm that kind of person in real life too. I try to see the best in situations, even in violence and war. I use a lot of guns and bullets, but they've been disarmed by being chopped up or ground to dust. When I went to the factory where they make poppies I found they're cut out of long sheets of red paper so you're left with yards of red paper with poppy-shaped holes in it. That for me is much more evocative than the poppies themselves. So I made a giant red tent out of the material. It was based on this famous gorgeous, sumptuous golden red tent called Pot of Gold, which Henry VIII took to France and put up for his peace summit with the French. What I especially liked was that the veterans in Manchester used it – they had a choir in it, it was the background for their calendar. When I was working with the police in Manchester I asked if I could use a sawn-off shotgun and they said fine, they just had to decommission it. I had been thinking of melting it but they chopped it into pieces and I found I liked the pieces. So I called the work 'Sawn-up, Sawn-off Shotgun' – once sawn by the criminals and once by the police.

I still have all the self-doubt I had when I was 16. I think it's just part of my makeup. The foundations I had weren't that secure so I always had the harpies on the shoulder saying you're not good enough, which was what my father said. You're a bit of a waster. You're not working hard enough. I've always worked really hard – that's my father doing that. In a way I wish I could step my foot off the pedal and relax but I have this need to keep reinventing the wheel. I'm never satisfied with anything I've done. I have suffered with depression throughout my life. It's the beast at the back of the cupboard. The work is important for that – it unleashes the beast and lets it rampage out in the world.

I'd like to tell my teenage self, don't worry, things get easier. I didn't think I was loveable when I was 16. I was a bit of an awkward misfit. I'd tell her it's never too late. I didn't meet my husband (Texan artist Jeff McMillan) till I was 40. I didn't have my child till I was 45. It wasn't planned but it was great. I got nominated for the Turner when I was 40. I still wasn't represented by a gallery at that point. I think I sabotaged a lot of things early on, but though I didn't have a great path, it ended up being the right path. If I'd had a child at 25, before I sorted my demons out, I'd have been a very fucked-up mother.

I've enjoyed being a mother, it's fantastic. Much more complex, much more of a creative thing than I'd thought. And a lot of fun. I think there's a whole chunk of your brain that's dormant, waiting for you to be a parent. You feel new things, in a different way than before. You feel more vulnerable. And it's been good for my own childhood crap. I can sort of go back and repair it and that has really been fantastic. Lily's childhood is the one I'd have liked for myself. And I'm so glad that I didn't miss out on motherhood.

If I could go back and relive any time, it would be 1997 when I met my husband in Texas. It's nearly 20 years ago now. He helped me pick up the pieces of wood for my 'Church Struck by Lightning' piece. He was a gentle giant, a calm, nice person, an artist, a few years younger than me. He was not phased by being with an older woman who was more successful. We had the same values, about doing what we want to do, being free, making art. I'd had a few boyfriends like my father – charismatic, manipulative. Jeff was not like my father. He knows who he is and he's a much-loved individual. Around the same time as I met him I had a phone call saying I'd been nominated for the Turner Prize. And the Frith Street Gallery called and said they'd like to represent me. So a lot of the problems I'd been having in my life – not having a life partner, not making money out of my work – were all resolved in just a few months in Texas.

Abi Morgan

Writer and producer
25 April 2022

I spent my childhood going from one area to the other. I went to seven schools because both my parents were in the theatre so we moved every few years. When I was 16, I was in Stoke on Trent, and the Potteries has many brilliant things about it, but I never thought I really fitted. So I was floundering when I was 16. I hated school with a vengeance and I didn't do well. About seven years ago I was diagnosed with adult ADHD, and that was revelatory for me, to suddenly understand why I found processing and systems and institutions incredibly difficult. Most of my memories of school involve sitting on the swings in the playground eating Kit-Kats after I signed in. I just walked out again. So I found school very hard but I had no idea what I might do next. I guess I just took a long time to grow into myself.

One thing I did know I loved when I was a teenager was television. The beautiful little box in the corner of the room that transported me to other worlds. Having a mother who probably played every Shakespeare part there was, I saw a lot of plays in the theatre – Shakespeare, Chekhov, Beckett, David Mamet. But what I loved about TV was the control I had – I could turn it off, I could move around the four channels. I loved *Grange Hill* then *Brookside* and *Coronation Street*, then the work of the British directors Jimmy McGovern and Ken Loach. That was my great escape really.

If you'd met the 16-year-old me you'd find her painful, gauche, trying to cope with huge boobs. Desperately trying to fit in but clearly incredibly awkward. But what I did do was, I chatted, I couldn't stop talking. I think you would have probably told me to shut up.

In terms of what I might do with my life, theatre and story-telling was the family business. I grew up with playwrights and actors and directors. I knew very quickly that I wasn't going to be an actress. I wanted something that gave me some sense of control and as an actor you always need someone who can give you a job. What I realised with writing very early on was that it was something I could do totally on my own. As a teenager I didn't yet know what I was going to do, but I knew I loved the world of storytelling. And I had to find a way of being part of it without being in front of the camera or on stage. When I went to university, writing became this incredible escape and I had the realisation that maybe this was how I could create and communicate with the world.

I still remember the first thing I wrote that got a real response. I loved the way Alan Bennett created character and the way he owned the screen for 30 minutes, so when we were asked at uni to write a monologue I thought, I can do this. I wrote a monologue about a woman I'd observed on a train one day – I'd been really fascinated because she'd taken a whole Iceberg lettuce out of her bag and spent the entire journey eating it. So I created a story that she'd silently cut this lettuce from her father's vegetable garden, and you realised it was about a woman escaping an abusive relationship and the eating of the lettuce was an act of defiance, a liberation. We had to perform the monologues ourselves, and whilst I'm no actress, one of the things I felt powerfully was the silence of the audience. It was exhilarating and surprising. And I had this profound sense of finding my North Star.

If I could go back and tell my younger self what happens in her future, I think she'd be surprised that she'd survived. She would be surprised that she had a currency beyond physical beauty. And that she'd grow into her ears and her boobs. And that one day she would lose one of those boobs; I had a mastectomy a couple of years ago (Abi revealed in 2020 she was recovering from breast cancer.) That, more than anything, reminded me of that desire to live. And I guess she'd be surprised that she'd raised a teenage daughter of her own, who she tried to teach the lessons she'd learned in the hope that her daughter would have more confidence and more self-belief in the world.

When I think of some of the men I worked with on those gig economy kind of jobs in my late teens, all the sleazy innuendos and sexual hassles that ran parallel with just being a young woman, I wish I'd learned to look those men in the eye and tell them to piss off. I wish I'd had more courage and the strength to know my own power. One of the things I've realised is that I've been guilty of just ignoring misogyny. But silence is compliance in a way. If I could go back to myself in my 20s I would walk up to that sleazy pizza delivery boss I worked for and say, go fuck yourself.

My book (autobiography *This is Not a Pity Memoir*, 2022) has been one of the hardest things to release out into the world. It was both a solace and a refuge, born out of a desperate need to communicate not only to myself, but to my partner who was in a coma and then for a long time, very absent from themselves (due to complications related to his MS medication, Abi's husband, actor Jacob Krichefski, was in a coma for several months, after which he struggled to remember her). I had a real compulsion to describe what it's like when you are in one of the loneliest places in the world and how you find yourself behaving in intense moments of crisis and how you survive them. When the life of the person you love most in the world and then your own life are put in jeopardy, the ability and the desire to swim as far away as you can from the current trying to pull you back is incredibly powerful.

I was surprised how humiliating I found vulnerability. I was surprised by how defiant my need and desire to live was. And I was humbled and moved by how essential it is to be vulnerable and to lean into other people helping you. I was blown away by the NHS. Each one of those components was absolutely essential. And not only to Jacob's survival, but also my survival and the survival of our family. I guess at a very simple level, I learned how strong I was.

If I could have one last conversation with anyone, I would choose my father. I would say I forgive you. And I would say I hope you forgive me. If you come from observing a toxic divorce, you realise that actually, the repercussions of that go on throughout your life. Now that I'm in a marriage of my own and I have children on my own I have more understanding and appreciation of the complexities of divorce. So I have a desire to build bridges rather than break them down.

If I could go back to any time in my life it would be when my children were little, to the festivals we went to on those long summer holidays. I just want to bottle that feeling because my children are getting bigger and they're going to have their own life and while there's great joy in that, it's a constant reminder that nothing is forever.

I remember one particular holiday in Costa Rica, in 2015. We went to an incredible beach party on New Year's Eve with music and fireworks and fire-eaters. At one point we broke away from the crowd and the four of us, Jacob, Jesse, Mabel and I, went off on our own to watch the fireworks explode across the bay. And we danced. I especially remember the dancing. It was heady and giddy, one of those rare moments when you're there, and you're in it, and you don't want to be anywhere else.

Chapter 3:

Self-belief

Shaparak Khorsandi

Comedian and author

1 September 2021

At the age of 16 I was extremely shy and quiet. I had very, very, very long, thick curly hair that I hid behind. I was very self-conscious about my weight. I couldn't talk to boys easily, I just sort of hung out with a few girlfriends, and went to a lot of indie discos. I only got four GCSEs, because I had undiagnosed ADHD and dyslexia, but I found a – complicated! – route to studying drama at college. Though I was shy, I was very determined to do that.

At that time racism was only talked about in the context of racial slurs. Or duffing people up in an alleyway. We didn't have the vocabulary we have now to describe the much more subtle racism that even the people who were harming us weren't aware that they were doing. It was either you were called the P word, or you weren't. It was a very, very difficult thing to bring up, when people were overtly racist towards you and called you slurs, there was a shame around it. I witnessed my parents getting it and it wasn't anything we ever talked about. It felt like there was no one to go to, to talk about how it felt, and that feels really awful when you're very young. It makes the world feel unsafe.

When I was 16 I made friends with a lovely gay boy in my area. And I remember a bunch of people came up to me and said, 'Do you know what he is?' That was the first time I saw homophobia, so at 16, I became quite a militant gay rights activist, that became my cause, my identity. I went to gay rights marches, Pride. I absolutely immersed myself in the gay cause, as we called it then. I went to university, and I joined the gay society, and came out as bisexual, which wasn't received well in the '90s I have to say – either in the straight community or the gay community – so I went straight back into that closet.

We felt in literal danger as children. In 1984, terrorists were sent over from the Islamic Republic of Iran to shoot my dad (exiled Iranian poet Hadi Khorsandi). The plot was foiled but that was quite a trauma. My dad was my absolute hero growing up. I was always being told how brave he was. He was very proud of me. He kept telling people, 'Shappi really cares about the gay people.' He was very proud that there were these people I was sticking up for, without understanding that I felt part of them.

It was a big deal for me to be a writer like my dad. The other day he was at my house, holding my book, *Kissing Emma*, in his hand, saying, 'Look at what you've done, you've written a whole book.' He doesn't have the concentration to write a novel. He understands things haven't always been easy for me. Sometimes he'll say, 'Shappi had no one to help her, she was a kid of two foreign people who were so consumed by what was happening in our own lives, we didn't have the time to navigate her through school, or understand that she had dyslexia and ADHD, we just left her to it.' It was really lovely to know that he saw that, because I think we all need a bit of validation from our parents, even when we're 48.

When I left university all my friends were getting jobs and I thought there was something wrong with me because I couldn't fill out a CV and I knew that whatever job I'd have, I would never have a boss. Not because I thought I knew better, but whenever I've had a boss, it made me feel really stupid and frustrated. I could never understand how to toe someone else's line. I never lasted in any jobs, I just couldn't focus. So I worked as a cleaner and a life model because those are jobs you can do while you're daydreaming. And I very much needed to be locked in daydreams. When I had kids, that was really difficult because children interrupt your daydreaming. Learning how to navigate that was quite a journey, let me tell you.

If I could go back to me at 16, I would tell her... oh, it makes me cry because it's been so hard not to be diagnosed till very late in my life. I would say to my 16-year old-self, you have a neurological condition called attention deficit disorder. That's why you failed your GCSEs. That's why you feel awkward socially, and that's why your decision making is so hard and doesn't adhere to any boundaries or values. ADHD is the reason why you will have bulimia, and why you will start to binge drink and have a bad relationship with alcohol because eating and drinking will be how you self-medicate to quieten down your mind. The proper way to quieten down your mind is with the help of the psychiatrists and a good therapist and medication. And then you will feel like you've come out of prison.

When I got married, my parents were disappointed. My dad didn't understand why I got married when we lived in England and you can easily co-habit. He wouldn't walk me down the aisle, because that tradition doesn't exist in Iran, and when I explained the significance, he said, 'So I give you away, like you're a cow? I'm not going to give you away, I can't, this isn't me.' And my parents, like all my friends, could see that I wasn't in the happiest place in that relationship. My best friend took me aside quietly when I was dating and said to me, 'Are you happy? Because you're not yourself around him.' But I ignored the fact that the man I was marrying had fundamentally different values to me. I went against my own values. And it ended in divorce.

The first thing that comes into my mind when I think of good things to tell my 16-year-old self is 'Guess what? We have a golden retriever! You got the dog you dreamed about.' And I'd also say to her, you are a professional stand-up comedian. That's what she wanted to do. I'd love to say to that anxious 16-year-old girl, who wasn't gregarious or confident – you did it. It was really fucking hard but you did it, and it's so much fun.

There are still people I meet and I can't believe I'm meeting them. I was at an awards ceremony after-show party once and I just stood and stared at Billy Connolly, because Billy Connolly and Richard Pryor, in my humble opinion, are the greatest comics ever. He saw me staring and he understood that giving a comic like me a moment of his time would give me a precious memory for the rest of my life. He came over with a chocolate-covered strawberry and said, 'I brought this for you', and we had a silly conversation about chocolate strawberries that lasted about 20 seconds. Then he kissed my hand and said, 'I've got to go now.' And off he went. And I thought that was the most humane, most compassionate thing, to understand how happy you can make someone by just saying hello to them. If I could tell my 16-year-old self that one day Billy Connolly's going to come over to you at a party and give you a chocolate-covered strawberry... that would be a very big deal for me.

If I could go back to one moment in my life it would be when I got an A in my English A level. We went down to the school and looked through the big results sheets pinned up in the hall. I was queuing to look at my marks, and a teacher came up to the girl next to me, face full of joy, and said, 'Emily, you got an A for French!' And Emily jumped up in the air and she was so happy. And I was like, oh my God, how wonderful! Imagine being able to go home and tell your mum that, imagine being the sort of person that gets an A. Then I looked at my English result and it said, A. And I thought, well, that's wrong, I'm looking at the wrong line. So I followed it with my finger. And it was an A. I'd never got an A before. I just couldn't believe it. I'd been told I was stupid and lazy all throughout my school years. Getting that A was like my certificate to prove that the people who told me that, they were wrong.

Sabrina Cohen-Hatton

Firefighter, psychologist and writer
26 August 2021

Sixteen was a difficult year for me, all the more difficult because it's the age when you have all of your ideas about what the future should look like, or what it could look like. And at that point in time, I was sleeping rough, without a roof over my head, without any knowledge of where I might be the next day, or where my next meal might be coming from. When I look back, I know really horrible things were about to happen to me. But if I was to speak to my younger self, I would just say – you're stronger than you think. And you're stronger than anyone else thinks. So don't let those negative sounds drown out your inner voice. Because it was really easy for that to happen. When you know people make assessments of you based on how you're presenting or your circumstances and they completely write you off, it's so easy to write yourself off.

My backstory is certainly not unique to me. My father died when I was nine and I was in a single-parent household with a mum who found it incredibly difficult to cope and struggled terribly with her mental health. We lived in abject poverty for several years as a result. When somebody goes to war with their demons, everyone around them gets hit by the shrapnel. We were in a really volatile situation by the time I was 15, a crisis point where it was just too much. My mum loved me dearly but she didn't have the capacity to be able to look after me properly. It was then that I started to sleep rough.

I sat my GSCEs when I was homeless and stashed my books in a box in a derelict building because I didn't want to alert social services by asking for a school locker. Eventually all my books were ripped up in that building by a proper neo-Nazi skinhead – he saw my surname Cohen on my grammar book and he attacked me, he put out a cigarette on my arm. He really went to town on me. It was a horrible experience. After that I kept my books in a box in the *Big Issue* office. And I kept studying. I think I saw qualifications as a ticket out of there. You can't control what life throws at you or even how you feel about it, frankly, but you can control what you do about it next. I didn't want to throw away all the work I'd put in just because life had thrown me a difficult hand. I got six As and three Bs. So better than I thought I'd do under the circumstances.

The school wasn't particularly supportive when I was going through the most difficult time. One teacher actually saw me selling *The Big Issue* magazine and he looked at me, looked down at his feet and crossed the road to try to avoid me. And I knew at that point, literally, nobody cared. I remember I just burst into tears, I was so upset. You could see people writing you off with their eyes, and it made you feel ashamed. I was quite surprised by how many people were rude or abusive. And as much as you tell yourself you don't care what people think, it's human nature to care. So it does become part of who you are and how you see yourself. But there was also a hardcore of people who were very kind, who took the time to stop and talk. I felt the simplest action of just asking my name re-humanised me after so many interactions that felt dehumanising.

Selling *The Big Issue* gave me that important feeling of earning, of having hard cash in my hand that I had spent eight hours that day earning. When you then go and use that money to buy something hot to eat – there was no better feeling, truly. You might be spending the night in a derelict building, pushing dirty needles out of the way so you could lie down to sleep. I remember stacking up old paint pots so if I was attacked, I could throw paint over that person to give me a few extra seconds to get away. But when you've been standing for hours in the cold and the rain, and you're soaking wet, and you go and buy yourself a hot coffee and hot toast – my God, that was so satisfying.

I remember one particular time around Christmas when I was huddled in a shop doorway on a high street with some other *Big Issue* vendors. All the Christmas decorations were up and everyone seemed to be happy and doing that Christmas thing, embodying the Christmas spirit. I don't think I'd ever felt so lonely or so sad. If I could go back in time I'd put my arm around myself at that moment and say, hey, you know, it'll be okay. And I'd remind myself about my dog, Menace. He was my stray dog for a stray girl. He was amazing. Dogs have always been a huge part of my life, giving me companionship and joy. I didn't have much but I always had Menace.

The reason I wanted to work for the Fire Service is because as a firefighter you're trusted to know what to do around people who are having the worst day of their lives. They are at rock bottom. They're desperate. They don't know what to do. They don't know who to turn to. And I felt like I could relate to that. I've felt all those feelings of despair and desperation and anxiety. I've experienced loss and learned in technicolor about the fragility of life. I think the pain of those losses actually made me a better person, it increased my capacity for love. So I wanted to help people. I think in a way, I wanted to rescue other people in a way that no one had been able to rescue me. That was why the Fire Service attracted me. And the amazing thing about the Fire Service is they saw past what on paper didn't present like a fantastic option. They took me on the strength of who they believed I could be. For me, that was something that was very special. It's become a philosophy I've tried to live by.

My academic work came out of a day I went to a fire where another firefighter had been quite severely burned and there was a one-in-four chance it was my husband. I was torn between the role of a loved one, with all the fears that go with that, and the role of a responsible responder. It wasn't him, but the experience got me looking at what we could do to make that situation better for people in the future. I found that 80 per cent of injuries across all industries, including the Fire Service, happen as a result of human error. So I did a psychology degree with the Open University, then I did a part-time PhD, both while I was still working full-time. I'd go into the lab at five o'clock in the morning, I'd run my experiment, I'd go to work about 8.30 for the full shift, go home, and put my newborn baby daughter to bed. I had seven years to do a part-time PhD, but in the end they registered me as a full-time student and I finished it in three.

If I could talk to anyone one last time it would be my dad, without a shadow of a doubt. He was so good-natured and so funny. And so so loving. The sky could fall down when you were with him and he wouldn't notice, you know, he was that kind of a dad. It was amazing, the way he dealt with his brain tumour. He never gave up. They told him he had six months, and he lived several years. He just kept fighting and defying all of the odds. He died when I was nine and we'd had this big argument the night before it happened. I went to bed being really belligerent, as usual, refusing to come down, and I stayed in bed and cried myself to sleep. Then I woke up and he was gone. That was a really painful lesson that I've carried with me forever. But I'll tell you what, I'll make damn sure it's never too late again. If I could have one more conversation with him I'd apologise for being such a little sod. And then I'd thank him for his influence, and for making me me.

Cyndi Lauper

Singer-songwriter

4 April 2016

At 16, I had just got a guitar and I was so excited. I had saved up a long time, and finally I had my guitar. I would stay up all night and sing and write and paint. I thought I was going to be a musician and I got a band together but they fell apart. And I was almost lost then, because if it hadn't been for music I didn't know what I would do. Sixteen was not easy for me. It wasn't so sweet. And a year later I really was lost.

My circumstances when I was a teenager were difficult. Maybe my personality didn't help me fit in either. By that point I couldn't take school anymore. I'd been in high school for seven years. I had been kept back so many times graduation felt like it was getting further and further away. I spent my time humming to myself. I was in the art class where they hand out rounded scissors to cut out paper. Nothing was connecting. It was very difficult. I didn't learn the same way as everyone else. I wasn't like them, though I wanted to be. So I became more of an outsider, wearing things and doing things that frightened the people who laughed at me. People are afraid of crazy people so I did crazy things to scare them and keep the assholes away. I was always a bit psycho, a mild schitz.

Before I was a pop star, I used to have people throw rocks at me 'cause I was wearing vintage clothing that didn't fit very well, and it was different. Someone threw a rock and I'd say, oh really? Where did you get your clothes from? A rack alongside ten others that were exactly the same? But then when I became famous everyone started dressing like me. I didn't expect that. I guess they just wanted to have fun. But I felt like I couldn't be who I was anymore because it had all gone. It was like a uniform, this thing I'd put on to empower myself. I'd picked out all those pieces. When we were doing the club scenes everybody had their own space. Madonna dressed her way, I dressed mine, and we didn't want to look like each other or anybody else.

If I met her now, I think I'd still like the younger me. Around 17, I worked out you have to like yourself. I would tell her things will work out fine. I'd say, your beginning might not have been so good, but you can start again now. And I'd say, don't be afraid. What would she think of me? I think she'd be proud of me. That I always stood up for what I believed in, even when my choices weren't popular.

The big changing point for me was when I joined a band. That's when I stopped being so odd; I'd found my tribe. Were they the quintessential end product of what I was going to be? No, but I was on my journey. I would tell my young self to learn to be patient. It would be a long journey but I was in it for the long haul. When you first join a band it's all for one and one for all. But as you go you realise, you know what, if the person next to you isn't going along with you, you have to go your own way.

I always knew I was born to be famous, but there's no handbook that tells you how to do it. It's a whirlwind. One thing: people are almost too nice to you and you can get away with all kinds of things. Two – you can't go out anymore because everyone jumps all over you. You can't even sit down and have dinner with someone outside your apartment. I found the whole love you hate you thing difficult. I couldn't deal with that kind of fame, when people go cuckoo over you. I like to go for a walk. I used to write when I was walking, so not being able to go for a walk really bothered me. On the other hand, fame allowed me to do my work, my art, and I learned how to do things I never would have otherwise. I'm very grateful for every single thing that happened to me. All the pitfalls teach you something, then you get back up and try again. That's how life is anyhow.

I have been criticised my whole career. My manager once said that I was like the Rodney Dangerfield of Music, until I wasn't. She meant that I didn't get the respect until later in my career and sometimes I'm not completely understood. But I've always walked to the beat of my drum. Sometimes I'm loved for it and sometimes I'm not.

Of course there have been times when I've lost faith in myself. I'm still fearful. But I say to myself, walk forward, keep walking forward. Don't do stupid, unsafe things, but don't be afraid to try things. I still make mistakes because, even in my sixties, I'm growing.

I always thought clothes were important. I wrote a song

once, 'Hatful of Stars' (1993, when she was 40) about this lucky hat I found. I don't know where the hell it is now, you lose things as you go. I was so lonely at that time. I had my dog. And I held the hat up to the sky and I imagined taking the sky and putting it in my hat. And every time I wore that hat I could close my eyes and see the sky.

I think I was happiest when I first had my son. Those first two months, to be that close to him. It was fun, playing with him, talking to him. And when he fell asleep I'd dress him up in all kinds of clothes and take pictures of him. That's the only time you can do that, when they're very little. After that they start having their own tastes. But those first six weeks, they are magical.

Alesha Dixon

Singer and television personality
20 February 2020

I was quite rebellious at 16 years old, and very sociable. I did like my clubbing. But I think when you're 16 you tend to carry the weight of the world on your shoulders, there's so much pressure to succeed. So I was also worried about my GCSEs and what path I was going to take. Fortunately for me, I always had quite a clear vision and even though I'm not doing now what I thought I should be doing – becoming a PE teacher – I was always one of these individuals that had a plan. I was an interesting mix between somebody who was a bit of a rebel, but also quite sensible and focused on making sure that I carved out a career for myself.

Lots of people describe my childhood as tough (her father moved away when she was four, and her mother suffered domestic violence from a subsequent partner). But I have great memories of being in a very loving household, with great friends and great family. Like lots of human beings I had challenging times and of course, everything you go through shapes who you are. So I was very streetwise as a kid, very savvy and awake to the world. I wasn't one of those 16-year-olds walking around in a whimsical fairy land. I had a strong grip on what the real world was like, but at the same time I was a dreamer. I dreamt about creating the life that I wanted. I dreamt about having a successful family. I dreamt about being on stage and travelling the world. So as much as I was a realist, I was also an optimist.

I've always had a good relationship with my mum. She was great at supporting my optimism. When I said to my mum I'm interested in singing or I'm thinking about joining a girl group, most parents would be freaked out by something like that. They'd tell you to get a sensible job. But she was always encouraging me, saying things like, it's very important when you wake up in the morning that you enjoy what you do, that you love what you do, because that's how you shine.

I remember when I told people I wanted to be a singer, I was aware almost as the words were falling out of my mouth how ridiculous it sounded. Because the music industry may as well have been on Mars. I knew nothing about it, it was such a far-fetched dream. But my mum always made me feel like anything's possible if you've got a vision. I think that's probably what helped me make the decision after two years of college to leave and pursue singing. It was a massive, massive risk but because I had that support, I was able to take that risk.

I've always been a very strong-headed, determined person. But I'm 41 and even though I've ticked lots of boxes, I still question the next ten years. What am I going to do next? I think when you're a creative person, you tend to live in that space of 'what's next?'. The unknown is quite an exciting place now that I don't fear it anymore. When I was younger I feared the unknown. I needed to know what was going to happen. Now I've accepted that a lot is out of my control. I can work towards things, but actually life is always surprising, so you've got to let go. Give it over to the universe.

My biggest riskiest decision was to leave Mis-Teeq (the successful all-female R&B/rap band she was in until 2005). I had been in a girl group for eight years. That was my comfort zone. But there was an instinct, a feeling towards the end of my time in the group that I wasn't happy. And I needed to leave. I was only 25, I hadn't paid off a mortgage, I still had bills to pay. So it was a major, major decision. I signed a new record deal and spent a year and a half making an album that the record company shelved, then found myself out of a deal. So I was like, oh my God, what have I done?

I would tell my younger self to have faith. There I was, sitting in my house with no record deal, having pretty much lost all the money I'd ever worked for, and some other things that were going on in my life that have been very publicly documented (her marriage to rapper MC Harvey broke off after his affair with another singer). I literally thought I'd lost everything. And then the universe just said, that's what you thought, but here we go. You're about to enter into this new phase of your life. And then I had a hugely successful solo record and had this incredible journey when in 2007 I became a contestant on *Strictly Come Dancing* and I won. And that took me on to becoming a judge on the show. The biggest risk brought the biggest payoff.

Music has always been top of the list for me, where I feel my most authentic self, where I feel the most happy. And yet it always ends up at the bottom of my schedule; there are all these obstacles. But what a brilliant problem to have, juggling all these amazing things. One day I'm working on my children's book, another day I'm working on the best show on TV (as a judge on *Britain's Got Talent*), then I go into the studio and have therapeutic writing sessions and pour my heart out into a song. But once I get back in the studio, I just feel so alive again and I feel so good and that's best of all.

Looking back now, when I was 16 I was so anxious. I wasted a lot of time worrying. I wish I could go back to that 16-year-old and tell her everything's going to be okay. And actually, failure is not a bad thing. When you're young you think, oh my God, if I fail it's the end of the world. You don't realise that actually, it might be the making of you. And I wish that back then I knew that challenging times and up-and-down moments are just the landscape of life. Sometimes when you're younger you have these idealistic takes in your head that everything should be smooth. But life comes with bumps in the road.

I've had lots of amazing moments but the best of all was probably when I got the phone call to be on *America's Got Talent* (she was a judge on *America's Got Talent: The Champions* in 2020). For about 20 years, maybe more, I've been obsessed with working in America. So that was the moment that really felt like a dream come true. Don't get me wrong, I've had many amazing moments, but what was so significant and exciting about the phone call that I got to be on *America's Got Talent* is that it happened when I was 40 years old. We have these pre-conceived ideas about what happens when you get to a certain age. And there I was at 40, getting the best phone call of my life. And oh, I happened to be pregnant at the same time too!

Alesha Dixon

If I could go back to any time in my life, I'd be onstage, probably at V Festival in 2009. It was a glorious sunny day. I looked out at this never-ending sea of humans singing my own songs back at me and I felt like I was standing on the top of the world. I remember feeling grateful in that moment. One thing I do like about my personality is that I've always been grateful and even at the very, very beginning of the Mis-Teeq days, I never took anything for granted. I've always known how lucky I was and I've just loved every minute of it.

Dame Steve Shirley

Businesswoman and philanthropist
25 June 2018

I think I was a bit of an odd teenager, desperately trying to conform. I do believe character is moulded very early in life. I was an unaccompanied (*kindertransport*) child refugee (sent from Germany to live in England in 1939) and that left me with a very odd childhood. I was five years old when I arrived. I was lucky because I was clutching the hand of my nine-year-old sister, poor thing, who had the responsibility of me as well. We had a new nationality, new food, new language, new parents. It was traumatic and it took me many years to get over that trauma. Literally, six years of analysis at a very good clinic. Because it really mucks your life up.

I remember someone saying to me, aren't you lucky to be saved. Which is not a healthy thing to say to a child. It left me with this strong feeling that I had to make something of my life, that I had to make sure the life that was saved was worth saving. Already in my teens I was beginning to get that serious intention that I mustn't fritter the day away. What was I going to do that day to make it worthwhile, how could I make it better than the day before? That feeling has stayed with me all my life, right up until today.

I think in my teens I was already starting to be charitable. I remember doing things to support a little animal charity. I was aware that so many strangers had given to me that I had to give back. I've done that all my life, whether it's advice, contacts or money. I didn't have much money until recently but those childhood motivators have never changed. Obviously I can get frivolous about clothes and things like that but I do know the spiritual side of life, the non-material things – the art, the literature, the friendship, the love – these are so important to me. I have tried to live a spiritual life. I don't think I would have been very happy if I hadn't given much of my money away (she has donated around £70million of her personal wealth). I could have had a lot of great paintings on the wall and a very nice wardrobe. But my husband wouldn't like that, and I don't think I'd have liked it either.

I had a lovely relationship with my foster parents. I am their child in all but birth. I had all their values. We were lucky in that both of my (biological) parents survived and we were reunited. I lived with my mother again for some years, but we never really bonded again. I was enormously proud, particularly of my father, who was a brilliant man. But I never really knew him as a person.

I went to a Roman Catholic primary school. The nuns were lay teachers, and the values they gave me were terrific. But they were sufficiently professional enough to say to my parents after a couple of years, look, your child is gifted in mathematics. We cannot teach her, she'll have to go somewhere else. So I got a scholarship and went to a very good grammar school. And I thrived there. It was intellectually challenging, I loved it. I would have loved to go to university but again, that wasn't really possible. We were poor and I needed to start making money.

When I was a teenager I was going to be the world's greatest mathematician. I was going to work in an academic environment and find out new theorems and theories. I did actually start work after school as a mathematical clerk, but I soon realised I didn't have it in me to do that sort of work. I was lucky that the computer industry came along and I really was able to contribute. I decided almost overnight, it's not maths, I'm going to work in computing.

When I started my company (Freelance Programmers), I was writing letters to promote it, telling people what we did. And I got no replies whatsoever. So my husband suggested I use the family name of Steve rather than the double feminine of Stephanie Shirley. And I began to get some replies and interviews and eventually things took off.

The culture when I started working was that women were not expected to do serious things. All the emphasis was on home and family responsibility. We weren't allowed to work in the Stock Exchange, we weren't allowed to fly an aeroplane. There was legislation to stop women working at night. As time went on I began to get really quite aggressive about it. Starting my company was part of a woman's crusade. Every survey we did told us women workers wanted flexibility and family-friendly work. So that's what I did. We all worked from home. We worked as a team. We helped each other out. I knew whose child had measles, whose marriage was in trouble. It was like a family company and it stayed like that for many years until there were thousands of us. We had profit sharing, and eventually when the company went public, 70 of the workers became millionaires.

My son (Giles) was autistic. I think now I'd tell my younger self to talk to other people more about the problems I had. Most of my colleagues didn't even know I had an autistic child. He was extremely difficult. He needed a lot of help. My sister came and lived with us with her daughter. Those were very tough times. For a long time I felt very much, why me? Am I not fit to have a healthy child? And it took two years for me to think, well, why not me? I'm able to fight for him. And so I did, and he did 'well' as the expression goes. He died 20 years ago (after an epileptic seizure when he was 35). I was very sad and I could hardly work. Sadly, my husband wasn't good at talking. Our son's name is hardly mentioned. Still. The death of a child is unbelievably painful. My husband has just not recovered. I think I have. I work for autism charities now and that pervades every part of my life. That's just my way of coping.

Imagine telling my younger self not only that one day I'd write a memoir of my own life but that it would be made into a film! I only hope I live long enough to see that film. We've just got a screenwriter and a producer – Joe Oppenheimer from the BBC. It's going to be good. Who would I choose to play me? Well, maybe I shouldn't say this, but they're talking about Emma Thompson! She's wonderful, isn't she? I know if she was in it, it would be really, really good.

I'm very comfortable in my old age. But if I could go back to any time in my life it would be early married life with a baby. I just could not believe how lucky I was. My marriage was a love match. We'd found a lovely little cottage in Buckinghamshire and I was doing it up. I was starting my company. I had this lovely placid little baby. It was perfect.

Chapter 4:

Inspiration

Sara Pascoe

Comedian

29 October 2020

At 16, I was sure that I was going to be an actor. I was very into amateur dramatics and going to drama club and auditioning. And I was a bit of a tearaway at the same time. So though drama club makes me sound very dweeby, most of the people at drama were a little older, so there was a lot of drinking in the park too. My mum tried desperately to keep me and my sisters inside but we were quite feral.

My dad moved out when I was seven. My parents were unhappy together so it was a relief when he left, they were both much happier. Until he moved to Australia when I was 16 we saw him regularly so he was very much still our dad. I remember later at school, meeting people who were sad about their parents divorcing, and I was thinking, no, it was brilliant, no arguing anymore. It was sad when my dad moved to Australia though. It did feel like I was never going to see him again because it's such a long way away. When I met an Australian man (her now husband, comedian Steen Raskopoulos) it was kind of my mum's worst nightmare: 'No, you are not moving to Australia.' I said, no, he's moving here. So I've done the opposite to my dad – he married an Australian, I've stolen an Australian back.

I was very sad when I was 16, but I didn't particularly know how to verbalise it. The reason I think I really loved acting at that time was I could pretend to be somebody else, not myself, a person I loathed. And also, I really thought that it would change everything if I became successful. So that's what I really focused on. It was a driving force for me, but I think it came from quite a negative place. I think it's a very typical teenage thing. I didn't like what I looked like. And I didn't feel very popular. It was just a disappointment in myself, thinking everyone else was having a good time, an easier time, and more boys fancied them. I was very jealous of other people, especially people who had money, who could afford to buy nice clothes and things like that. I always found that very hard.

I look back at myself and think, she was so young and thin! You just get older and fatter, and you look back at old photos and think, she hated herself so much. It's crazy. Sometimes because of my job now I get to talk to young people, and it's so hard because when they reach out because they're unhappy you think, I absolutely know how you feel. Because in that moment it feels like life or death, and you're crying yourself to sleep because someone said you've got a big nose. You feel it very deeply.

If you met the 16-year-old me, you'd think I was very confident. I'm actually more confident now but back then I was that kind of cocky confident. I absolutely believed I was right about everything. I had very strong opinions. No deviating, no seeing things from other people's point of view. My dad is an interesting philosophical person and he told me when I was quite young, your teachers aren't always right, question everything. I think I was a bit disrespectful to some people. Of course as empathy grows you learn more about being a respectful human being. But I sometimes envy how sure teenagers are of things, just because they haven't had that much information.

One of the things the younger me got wrong is, I had a very stupid opinion for a long time about therapy. That you shouldn't try to be happier or solve your problems because that's where your creativity comes from. You're supposed to be miserable because that drives you to be more successful and work harder. And I saw therapy as a middle-class, namby pamby thing; oh my God, paying money to be listened to, how dare you! But that was really wrong of me. If I could go back I'd say everyone should have access to therapy. It's not about feeling sorry for yourself and being happier isn't some bourgeois narcissism, it actually means you're more able to be kind to other people. I really wish I'd realised that in my early 20s.

I think the idea of having money, having my own flat, and having a dog would blow the mind of my teenage self. The absolute ideal picture I had for adulthood was pets, having a bike, being able to eat whatever I wanted and especially having money. It completely changes your life. When I was in university I was heavily in debt because of university fees. Then I had to have a voluntary bankruptcy. I had years and years of paying that off, £20 a month. That's a cloud that lives over you, and it affects every single moment of your life. You think of it every morning as soon as you open your eyes. Still every month I look at my bank balance and I work out how many months I'd be able to survive without getting a proper job if the work suddenly stopped.

Having a dog is one of the things my younger self would be very happy about. It's the best thing, it's a love story. Yesterday I gave my dog a bath and afterwards he was shivering, so I put a blanket over him and he fell asleep on me. I didn't move for three hours because I didn't want to wake him up. There were so many things that I could have been doing but I thought, no, I'm just going to lie under a dog, not looking at anything, just feeling very happy. I think there's something special about love that's not based on language, it's such a different kind of intimacy. Human intimacy we kind of construct and you can't quite trust it, or it might change. Your dog could never do anything to make you think, oh, that's not who I thought you were. You get each other in a completely different way. And being outside with them and watching them leaping, running, jumping – I feel like that's my heart leaping and running across the grass, in the bushes, through the trees.

My advice to my younger self in terms of relationships is, when you're chasing... I don't want to say the wrong kind of people because that's not fair, but a toxic relationship, sometimes what you're really doing is trying to beat the feeling of rejection. 'They don't quite like me but if I can get them to like me, I'll feel better about myself'. It's really hard to break out of that cycle, because it's really compulsive, and you never really question if you like the person. It's just that when they don't like you, that feels so bad. A few years ago my friend who is happily married said, 'When you meet the right person it's easy.' And I didn't believe her. I remember thinking, oh, okay, boring, going out shopping for duvets and wallpaper, having conversations about cutlery, boring. And then when I met my partner it suddenly made sense. I kept thinking, shouldn't I be insecure about something, shouldn't I be worrying about something? Why am I not pretending to be someone else so that he'll like me?

I remember my big break moment really clearly. I'd done a stand-up gig for a competition called Funny Women in The Stand in London and the next day an agent who had been in the audience wrote to me and said, 'We'd like to have a meeting about representation.' She's the most incredible agent, she looks after people like Simon Pegg, and at the time, Catherine Tate, and David Schwimmer, all of these incredible people. We went out for a meeting and she agreed to take me on. I remember being on the phone to my dad when I was on a coach afterwards and he started crying because he was so happy for me. Looking back, I realise it was because I'd met someone brilliant who got it, who got me. She really was the first person who really believed in me doing a job. That was a big moment. I felt this kind of fizziness, a feeling of hope. It's going to be okay, I'm going to do this. Adulthood is going to be fine.

Mica Paris

Singer and actor
29 June 2020

My grandparents raised me in South London and I grew up in the church. I went seven days a week, it was very intense. So my childhood was full of lots of music and lots of Jesus. You say that to people and it sounds shocking. But actually it was really good. Pentecostal churches are very much community based and as I could sing, I was the star of the church from a very early age. At every gospel concert, church service, I was called to sing. And I saw the amazed reaction of the people. Even at nine, I knew if I held that note really long, I was going to get that effect. That was my thing. When a kid sees that they've got a trick, a special something that makes everyone glued to them, they're going to want to do it again and again. So then I started to become quite popular in the Pentecostal Church, which is a huge organisation. My grandmother and grandfather, they were just so proud of me. They used to take me all around the country.

Mica Paris

I was very driven at 16. All my friends at school were getting pregnant, getting up to all sorts. And I remember thinking, oh my gosh, that's the worst thing that could ever happen. My grandparents were very proud Jamaicans. They came over to the UK with the *Windrush* and they worked very hard to get us a five-bedroom Victorian house. They instilled in me, you never sign on, you must work. So being raised in that environment, with the church and all of that, my ethics were about having your independence and making your own money and not relying on anyone else. That was at odds with the kids that went to my school. Lots of them, their ambition was to sign on as fast as possible. Get that flat. Usually that meant having a kid, because if you had a kid you'd get a flat even quicker. That was the modus operandi for them but for me, that was just horror.

I left the church when I was 16, and my grandparents were mortified. It was a very, very tough struggle because remember I was the star of the church at that time. But in the years leading up to my leaving, my parents came to pick me up at weekends and my dad would play stuff in the car like Marvin Gaye and the Isley Brothers (Motown music stars of the '60s and '70s). And I thought, I have to change the music. I love gospel, it's great, but I want to do that instead. So I'd been secretly listening to people like Marvin Gaye for years and then, oh my gosh, Prince came out. I had to hide his albums under my bed because they had women in G-strings on them. When I got to 16, I was already doing backing vocal sessions for bands and I was ready for a change in my life. I left the church and I moved to Brixton to live with my sister. My grandparents were traumatised.

Looking back, of course I was very selfish then, like every

teenager. But I made peace with my grandparents many years ago. They were the most incredible people. When I was just 19, my first record ('My One Temptation', 1988) blew up and everything went mental. I went to number seven in the charts, and my grandparents saw me on the telly. And they said, well, you know, she was right. Bless them, they used to wear my merch. They were so cute. They were just great people. People have always asked me, why didn't you go down that mad route and mess up yourself? And it really was because of them. They were so terrified about what might happen to me in the music industry, I wanted to prove to them that you can be in this business and not be a car crash. You can actually survive this thing, though yeah, it is a bitch.

My first experience of even thinking about race was when I saw the TV show *Roots*, when I was about nine. We were all glued to it. But as a child, I just didn't think about it much at all. Our family was very mixed. Jamaican people are very, very multicultural normally, because Caribbean countries are very mixed. At school there was a big mixture – Indian, Scottish, Irish, everybody. That's multicultural Britain. So as a kid, I didn't experience racism. But I have experienced it in my whole career. We'd have to sit here from now to June next year for me to tell you all the racist experiences I've had in my life. But I don't believe in this victimisation thing, always talking about it, because that's not constructive. I managed to forge a career regardless of those factors which are very much in existence in every aspect of my industry.

I had a few clashes with my record label about my weight. When I was a teenager, I was very tall and leggy – I'm five foot ten. Then later, at the height of my career, I got married to an Irishman and had a baby. And that's when I put on weight for the first time, as most women do. And I went back to the record company to talk about the next record and they said, you look like two people in one body. Do you know what size I was? I was a 14. It was ridiculous but at the time you're just thinking, I've got to make my career great. So I started training and in two months it dropped off. If you see the album cover just after that, I have my bathing suit on. I never saw that happen to male artists. The pressure that women are under – and then there's my race on top of that. That's what I've been battling my whole life. You just have to fight harder. It's a very male dominated business. And those men have a very idealistic vision of what a woman should be. They don't want you to speak in a certain way, they don't want you to show intelligence. As a young artist, I had so many clashes with my label, because I'm very feisty. I'd just say, no, I'm not having it.

The thing I would say to my 16-year-old self is, you have no idea how right your grandparents are about the industry. It is like hell. They were so right about that. It was hardcore, it is really tough. Thank goodness for my kids. They keep you straight, man, they make me want to be a better person. They centred me in the madness of this industry. It's up, down, up, down, and it's very hard to survive. You have to consistently fight off everybody who's trying to rip you off. You have to fight for your product to come out after you've spent so long making it. You have to be really passionate. Putting out a record, I always say it's like being in Tesco at six in the evening, naked. Imagine that, because that's what it really feels like when you put up a record that you've done yourself. It's the most scary thing.

I credit being brought up in the church for getting me

through the loss of my brother (in 2001 Jason, a postman, was shot dead). This is the beautiful thing about church; it taught me to be selfless. About the importance of people looking after each other. When my brother went through that – and it was horrific – well, my very first thought was about trying to keep my mum from jumping in the grave with him. Because she was destroyed. So we were trying really hard not to lose her as well. After that my first instinct was, we've got to help other people who have gone through the same thing. I had a lot of publicity about it, so I used that platform and I found out about this thing called Trident (a Met Police anti gun-crime operation, which Mica has been an ambassador for since 2001). That's where I met all these mothers who'd had similar things happen to them. And it was so healing. And this is what I tell people all the time; when you're going through any kind of crap, go and help someone go through their crap. It really helped me. You just can't do it on your own.

Monica Ali

Author

26 January 2022

My big preoccupation at 16 was getting out. We lived in a housing association estate and we had no money. I got a free place at the local private school and I became focused on education and saw university as my way out. At home it was quite difficult. I had to do a lot of sneaking around to go out and go to parties and go drinking and so on. There were a lot of secrets and lies and rows and tension – between my parents and between me and my father. I just wanted to have my freedom and that was a source of conflict. If you met the 16-year-old Monica you'd think she was confident, outgoing, up for a good time, desperate to be cool. Looking back, I think I was in a state of hyper vigilance the whole time. There were two things that made me always on the lookout – skin colour and poverty. Living on the estate, I was always on the alert. Because this was the late '70s going into the '80s and the tail end of the National Front. There was still a lot of graffiti around. I certainly didn't think of myself consciously as working that hard to fit in, but looking back, I was, I really was. And fitting in is actually the opposite of belonging. You need to make the effort.

I never thought I'd be a writer but reading was huge in my life. Jane Austen, Tolstoy, Flaubert, Zola. All that melodrama! I could always escape into a book. I think reading sort of saved me really. Because I could become deeply involved in a novel and be transported. I can't quite lose myself in a novel now the way I could as an adolescent, but writing does that now for me. It's a kind of oblivion. There are still times when I can't get there and it's really frustrating and I can't sink into it, I can't get into that flow state. But then the world falls away and I fall away and I love that, that sort of altered state.

If you'd told me at the age of 16 that I was going to be a writer I'd tell you, you were insane. Up until I read *The Buddha of Suburbia* (the 1990 Hanif Kureishi novel) in my early twenties I didn't have the faintest idea that might be something that I could do. And even then, it took me some more years to actually have the guts to try it. It was after I had two children, my daughter who was a baby and my son who was two. My grandfather died and we went to the funeral and we happened to have already booked this little holiday in the Lake District the next day. And I was carrying this galvanising feeling that you only have one life, so you've got to try the things that you really want to do. So I sat down and my husband took the children out for a couple of hours and I started what became *Brick Lane*. Until then I didn't know what I wanted to do other than get a job, earn money, live my own life, have a garden, that sort of thing. I thought about the civil service, maybe becoming a lawyer, because I was good at arguing. But actually, I didn't really want to do any of those jobs.

People often asked me how I managed to write *Brick Lane* with two young children always around, and I'd say oh, you know, it was fine. I could write when they slept. But looking back, I was deluding myself. It was really hard. But the other hand, once I got started it actually all happened really quickly. A friend who worked in publishing showed the first three chapters to her editor – I didn't think anything of it really. Then I got a call from the editor saying, have you got any more? I sent the other two chapters and then I got another call saying, we want to make you an offer.

It was so unexpected. Because this was a novel about a Bangladeshi housewife who spoke hardly any English. There was no reason whatsoever for me to think there would be any interest or appetite for it. Things have changed a bit since, but 20 years ago that sounded like a ludicrous proposition for a 'hit'. So when I got that phone call it was very exciting – I did do a jig around the house. It didn't seem real. But then I began to feel a bit anxious in case it put me off my stride, people looking over my shoulder. But actually, as soon as I got back to the writing, I didn't feel that at all. It made no difference.

If I could give advice to my younger self, I'd tell her to go to therapy much sooner in life. I remember laughing when my therapist called certain things that had happened to me trauma. I hadn't been beaten or abused. So it took me a while to understand and accept what she meant by that and to understand my tendency towards minimising events in my life. I'd also tell my younger self to get into meditation much sooner in life. A few years ago, I tried a mantra-based meditation and it was life-changing. It really helped me be kinder to myself.

You have to have a core of self-belief to be a writer. I think that was there for me from quite a young age, but then I lost it. This is the first book (*Love Marriage*) I've published in ten years. Because ten years ago I stopped writing. And then I got depressed. And then the depression made me less able to write and then came this downward spiral. I lost my confidence.

It's hard to explain what happened but I had a bit of a problem dealing with the reaction to my next books. Because I didn't continue writing *Brick Lane* part two, part three, etc. I wrote about whatever interested me. So I wrote *Alentejo Blue*, about an area that I know really well in Portugal. And then I wrote *In the Kitchen*, which was based in London and Lancashire, in a mill town not too dissimilar to the one I grew up in. Then I wrote *Untold Story*, about a fictional princess (the character was taken to be Princess Diana).

I think I was really naive in thinking that I could write about whatever I wanted, like a black or white male writer can. The response was bafflement. I remember one critic saying about *Untold Story*, 'a curious marriage of subjects and author'. People would ask, are you trying to get away from something? To me the question they really seemed to be asking was, are you trying to get away from brown people? Are you trying to get away from your ethnicity? I understand that it confused people but my mum's white, my father's Bengali. I was born in Dhaka, but I've lived here all my life. So, to me I was being entirely true to who I am. It's taken me a lot of therapy to understand that for me, that reaction felt like a kind of obliteration of the self. That sounds like hyperbole, but actually, I'm not exaggerating; this idea that I have to choose to be one thing or the other – it's existential. I'm not one thing or the other, I'm both. And I'm glad to be both. So

I think that critical reaction made me feel things which went very deep, which led to the loss of confidence and depression and all of that.

If I could go back to any point in my life, it would be when the kids were little. We used to have this house in Alentejo in Portugal, very rural. I would spend long summers out there, and friends would come and go, my husband would come and go. It was really dusty, that red dust which is very common out there, and the kids would roll around and cover themselves in this red mud. And then at the end of the day, just as the sun was going down, I would get the hose out and hose them down. And they'd be shrieking and jumping in and out of the spray. And it was just lovely. I would happily go back to that time.

Jo Whiley

Radio and TV presenter
9 July 2012

When I was 16 I was still caught up with my swimming, though truthfully I'd probably peaked when I was about 14. I was probably coming to terms with the idea that I was never going to be in the Olympics, but I was still training regularly. When I was swimming I felt like I belonged and I really knew myself. There had been a brief time when I'd got lots of attention and I saw that glint in my coach's eye – maybe this could be the one. But then boys and drink came along and I realised that was never going to happen.

I was never cool. Some girls at school wore make-up and had cleavages and knew how to show them off. That was never me, I was a bit blokey. I wore clumpy boots and ankle boots. I looked at the cool kids who went to gigs and tried to ride on their coat tails. I had a perm – oh God it was like ringlets around my head. I remember I was going out with a boy and I got my perm and then he met me at lunchtime the next day and said it's over; I knew it was the perm. I don't think we ever kissed or held hands but we were technically 'going out' and the hair interrupted it. I remember everyone going to see The Smiths (the seminal '80s indie band) but I went to the Thompson Twins (the '80s pop band) – bad choice. I'd tell the teenage me to be more daring, have a bit more confidence in yourself. I don't think I was very attractive and I didn't have a dazzling personality that made me stand out, I was just really normal and quite shy.

I grew up with just my sister Frances, who has cri du chat (a developmental and behavioural disability) and though I had friends, it was all really about family. All my parents' friends had kids with disabilities and some were a lot worse than my sister, so I grew up looking out for other people, always aware that some people found life really, really hard. I think it made me more sensitive and I think that still shows in my kids who are very considerate, as they've grown up with an aunt with a disability.

I owe everything to (ex-Radio 1 controller) Matthew Bannister. I'll never forget the day he called me and (fellow DJ) Steve Lamacq into his office at Radio 1. We'd been trying out, making pilots, but we had no idea if he'd ever employ us. He was starting the revolution that cleared out Dave Lee Travis and Simon Bates and those guys. We went in and sat down and he said, 'I'd like both of you to be part of Radio 1's future'. That was the *Sliding Doors* turning point in my life. I think Steve and I went down the pub for cider and peanuts but inside I was screaming 'Oh my fucking God, this is amazing!'

I've always felt comfortable behind a radio microphone but I've got nervous a few times in the past. Covering the massive Live 8 concert with Jonathan Ross and Fearne Cotton, that was just so huge it was like an out-of-body experience and I remember feeling rigid with fear and not being particularly good. I watch myself on TV as rarely as possible – when I do, it's very painful. I just sit thinking, I definitely shouldn't have said that.

If I could advise my young self starting out in radio, I'd tell myself the person you're interviewing, nine times out of ten, doesn't want to be there. If you fawn all over them they won't respect you and they'll eat you alive. My worst experience was probably Russell Crowe. He had just had a baby and I took a babygro in as a present – he just looked at it and said, 'Yeah, cheers, love', and threw it on the floor!

As I've got older I care less and less what people think of me and that's made me more confident. I think you do get to a point where you think, oh God, I'm getting older, but I'm past that now. I really don't care and I'm very happy in my skin. Anyway, if I ever raise the subject of Botox my kids and husband just give me such a hard time I wouldn't dare. And I see so many people who have tried fillers and pillow faces and now we're seeing the awful effects and I think, thank God I didn't go down that route.

The 16-year-old me, sitting in the upper sixth common room listening to U2, would not in a million years believe that one day she'd be going drinking around Dublin with Bono. I never dreamt of this life, I knew nothing about showbiz or radio, so if you told me one day I'd be co-presenting a show with Madonna, I would just have laughed. As for the fashion icon thing – ha ha!

I would never have thought I'd have four children but it was just such a revelation how much fun children are and how brilliant family life is. Once I'd started I didn't want to stop.

Jo Whiley

I'm so lucky to have had the absolute luxury of having a baby later in life. I genuinely would prefer to sit watching the US sitcom *Modern Family* with my four children and my husband on a Friday night than do anything else in the world, except maybe hanging out in Lake Como with George Clooney.

KT Tunstall

Singer-songwriter
4 December 2020

Sixteen was a really pivotal moment for me. From the age of eight I'd been in love with theatre and at 16, I was in a little theatre group in St Andrews, Byre Theatre, and I'd been accepted into the Scottish Youth Theatre in Glasgow. But suddenly I had this epiphany that I didn't want to be told what to do. I didn't want someone else to be writing the words or a director telling me what to do. I wanted to create my own stuff and be my own boss. I was a bit defiant, a bit weird, as a kid, a bit of a dreamer. So when we had a party at the end of a production and everyone was asked to do a little skit, I played a song instead. It was the first time I'd ever played a song for people after I taught myself guitar. And, it was like, whoa, that went down well! So that was a really pivotal moment of realising, actually, I'm not going to go into theatre, I want to be a musician.

When I was 16, I played my first gig in the Vic pub in

St Andrews. It was at 6 o'clock before the punters came in – I was underage but they let me play a little gig in the back room. And prolific singer-songwriter King Creosote, Kenny Anderson, came. He has kept a journal of every day of his life and I recently had the pleasure of sitting with him and going through it, and he showed me the diary entry he wrote in 1992 after seeing me play. It said, 'I've just seen this girl called Kate at The Vic. She's so talented. I think she's got something amazing. And I'm going to ask her to join the band'. So I immediately joined his band, the Skuobhie Dubh Orchestra, and started going around Scotland in a freezing transit van with them, much to my parents' frightened faces. They were like a bunch of Fife anarchists. They were living in weird little unheated cottages on the edge of town, just surviving, being musicians and nothing else. They didn't really believe in record deals and they didn't trust the music industry. So I kind of moved in and grew up with that mentality as well.

I have realised now, in middle life, how significant a role being adopted has played in the rest of my life. Jackie Kay, the poet (who is adopted), has that beautiful poem where she says there's 'always a little windy place inside'. And that is just the truth of it. I had kind of breezed over it for years, until my forties. Then I did that amazing programme, *Long Lost Families*, and found sisters. And they're just gorgeous, beautiful, fierce women. And we really do still just stare at each other going, oh my God, we look the same. We're very close in age and we grew up 15 miles apart. They were in Dunfermline and I was in St Andrews. They remember going to St Andrews at weekends, when I was working in an ice cream shop. And I was like, oh my God, I probably served you a cone!

It was funny because I met my biological mother, thinking I'd look just like her and she'd be an amazing singer or something. But no, neither. But the first thing she said to me was, you couldn't pass your father on the street. He was Irish, and apparently a fantastic singer. So it seems like that's where it's come from. But it's a strange feeling because at the end of the day, these aren't people I know. The way that I describe it, which feels most helpful to me, is that it has enriched my life because it's really good for the soul to be able to put faces and characters and meaning into those two blank corners. But you run a risk. These are human beings. And once you go down that road you can't really go back. But I'm really glad I took the risk. It's not been a bed of roses the whole time of course, but I'm glad I know.

I think the thing that would surprise the teenage me the most is that I would say, you're going to have the best time when you get into your 40s. It's not gonna happen in your 20s. It's not gonna happen in your 30s, even though that's when, quote unquote, all your dreams come true. But actually, it's the inner peace I've got to in my 40s that's allowed me to enjoy everything in a way that I couldn't through my 20s and 30s. I was a sensitive little soul, and I still am. So I would say to my younger self, it's alright to be a fuckup, it's alright to be a mess. Just don't pretend to be anything that you're not.

That's why I loved that Dolly Parton interview (in *The Big Issue*) because being a rock star, everybody wants a certain version of you, you know? And it's just great now at this point in life to realise, as she said, that actually, the most purposeful thing to be doing is absolutely being yourself. Being the same as anyone else is just a waste of time. If you're trying to be Chrissie Hynde (lead singer of US band, The Pretenders), don't bother. She's done it much better than anyone else is gonna do it. It's okay to just be yourself.

I would tell that young girl, the young me, stick to your guns, use your gut and don't hold it all in when you're feeling upset. I think there was an element of self-sabotage in the way I handled things because I didn't really like being famous. It really was a case of overnight success – after I did *Later with … Jools Holland* (the BBC music TV show) in 2004 everything changed. It went crazy. I was never a magazine cover artist, and I didn't really want to be and that's not very helpful if you want to be a rock star. So I didn't really use the power I had. I remember telling myself, nothing will really change. But of course it did. Everybody hanging on tenterhooks waiting to see where your next album is going to chart. Being told I couldn't delay my second record because it was going to make somebody's share prices drop. That's not what I wanted.

If I could have one last conversation with anybody, I wouldn't mind a half-hour sit down with a guy who completely broke my heart at 18. Again, I didn't realise until I was older how much it messed me up. Actually it was during lockdown – I did a writing session with Richie Sambora (US songwriter and lead guitarist of rock band Bon Jovi until 2013) which was absolutely incredible. And I wrote a song about it, called 'Breaking in a Brand New Broken Heart'. Because I had this habit growing up of wearing totally rose-tinted glasses, and never looking at the difficult part of things. I didn't want to handle it. Now I'd love to get that boy's side of it, and try to understand the complexity of that situation. It felt like a simple 18-year-old heartbreak to me. But actually, it was major. You're so tender at that age, you're on the cusp of creating yourself as an adult. It might be why I decided I didn't want to have a family.

If I could go back and relive any moment in my life, I would go back to the BRIT Awards in 2006. It had been such a long road, and really tough with my family, too. They'd been very worried about me. We were at odds for a long time because I was pursuing this career they just didn't think was going to work. But they were at the BRITs with me, I have this amazing photo of my dad – he's passed away now – but in this photo he has this really smug smile on his face, holding my BRIT above his head. Prince (the legendary US singer-songwriter) was playing, and my mum turned to me, and she goes, he's good, isn't he? I met all these incredible artists that I loved. And I won the category I was in alongside Kate Bush and PJ Harvey! I said I was gonna break the head off and give it to Kate Bush. And I met Jimmy Page (guitarist from the seminal rock band Led Zeppelin) and he said he loved my boots. What an amazing, amazing night and I had such a good time. I'd love to do it all again.

Chapter 5:

Independence

Billie Piper

Actor

2 March 2021

In my early teens I was at a theatre school in London, Sylvia Young, with the intention of becoming an actor. I became the face of the *Smash Hits* relaunch in the mid-'90s, and I had a series of commercials running in tandem. Hugh Goldsmith (managing director of Innocent Records, who launched his Virgin-affiliate label with Billie's 'Because We Want To'), asked me to make a demo which went well because I loved singing. I didn't think I was a great singer but I could definitely hold a tune. Then, I don't know how long after that – it felt like overnight, I have no concept of timeframe around those years of my life – he signed me. And I started just doing live shows.

By the time I was 16 I had left Swindon and was living in London, on my own. I was in a hotel in Maida Vale at first then I got together with this guy who had a flat in Kilburn, and I wanted to move in with him because I was lonely. I was working every day for up to 18 hours a day, living on a diet of garage food and takeaways. I was obsessed with music so I was living for MTV or The Box, they were constantly on a loop on my TV. I wasn't fully reclusive by that stage, I still had energy and a desire to be part of the world. I'd been working for two solid years, but I was still in a slightly more positive place than I'd be two years later. I think, in my own small person head, I felt equipped to live that life at 16. And maybe I was practically, but not emotionally.

Those teenage years are a period of my life that I'm reflecting on now for the first time in my adult life. And there's a lot of missing pieces to be honest, which I think speaks for itself. Those first few years were totally thrilling, and I just felt like I was living a dream of mine. But I was often in very strange, very adult situations that I wouldn't subject my own kids to at 16. Actually, my real takeaway from my 16th year is just how exhausted I was, because I was a teenager going through everything a teenager goes through but very publicly. With a schedule which would rival a high-flying businessperson. It must have looked peculiar from the outside, but I was having fun at that point, so I couldn't feel what that really meant. And I certainly normalised it very quickly.

It wasn't too long before that pop star life just stopped sitting well. I was absolutely burnt out and my love of performing was non-existent. I wanted to have a normal life. And I missed acting. There were a few things happening. One of the things I'd got so used to was having number one records and a high level of success. Then I had a single that didn't chart well and I remember thinking that it was the biggest failure ever. And at the same time I was sort of personally unravelling. That combination led me to think I needed some time off to re-evaluate what I want to do. I was so sick of doing what people wanted me to do. All of this thinking was subconscious, I'm not sure how aware of those moods I was, but that's what I ended up doing. Thank God.

I got into a meaningful relationship at that difficult time, where there was encouragement to prioritise myself for a while. So that was very helpful. My time with Chris Evans (the radio DJ to whom she was married from 2001 to 2007) was partly parties and pubs, but it was also another education in many ways. It felt like my university years, in the sense that I was meeting all these different people. I was living my life without a schedule, and I was learning a lot from it. Also, I was with someone who was incredibly optimistic and wilful, and definitely operating in a way that was very aspirational. Someone who knew what he wanted. And that felt very new to me, to be honest. I'd always seen people working for other people. He seemed to be working for himself, on his own path, with big intentions. That was quite inspiring.

Always in my head, the whole time throughout the singing career, was my hope to be an actor. In fact, that's why I decided to go with the singing career, because I felt like it would open doors for me in the future. And also I got to perform, which I loved. So the acting ambition was always there, it was just a question of when there would be confidence to rebuild. I had to go and do lots of lessons and training again. And then it was just a case of getting an agent and going to castings and being horribly rejected over and over. Having to prove myself twice as hard because people felt like they already knew everything about me as a person. And I think at that point I had quite a reckless reputation. So there was a lot of f*cking legwork.

I felt really emotional when I got the job as Rose in the

revival of the much-loved sci-fi series *Doctor Who*. I took my nan out for high tea in London, and I told her, and then it felt really real. Because we had a very close relationship and she knew I had this passion for acting. It was super-thrilling, exciting, and very moving for me because I wasn't sure about which way my life would go. I didn't know if I was going to go back to normal life after my singing career, a life where I wasn't pursuing the things I want to pursue.

If I'm at convention they often show 'Doomsday' (the *Doctor Who* episode which saw the final parting between Rose and The Doctor) before they introduce me on stage, and I find it so upsetting. I remember what it meant to me. It all felt very big. On a personal level I had become very close to David (Tennant) and we'd been through something very big together. I was sad about losing a sort of everyday friendship. Also, I think Russell (T Davies) writes in such a way that you can't help but be moved by his writing. There's this sort of 'life will out' spirit coursing through all of his work which is very moving. That episode marks me choosing to walk away from something that had been really significant and integral in my life and I was quite nervous about that. And as well as leaving the show, I was moving back to London into my own flat, Chris and I had separated – what was I going to do next?

I would love to go back to my former self and say, none of this matters. You're amazing, you're going to do just fine. Therapy has been crucial to my getting better, so I'd tell my young self to get a therapist. I just don't know how young kids cope anymore, I really don't. I think everyone's super-anxious, or at least that's how it feels to me. If you can get your kids any sort of mental health support or family therapy, just get it. There's no shame in it whatsoever. When I think of characters like Suzy and Mandy (from the TV show *I Hate Suzie*, and the Piper-directed film *Rare Beasts*), they might have had quite different lives if they'd had therapy.

If I could go back and have one more conversation in my younger days, I think I'd go back to pre-fame years with my mum and dad. Because I think everyone's relationship really took a hit during those years, and it would be nice to go back and reflect on that, in a way that was much more focused. We had little contact and a strange sort of arm's-length relationship which is fine now, but if I could, I would go back and prepare us all more for that.

If I could go back and relive any time in my life, I would go back to my very early teens, just out of Year 7, going into Year 8, when I had full anonymity. No paranoia about everyone knowing who you are. I'd just hold on to those moments with my mates, driving around in boy racer cars, Oasis or The Prodigy playing on the radio. Smoking fags. Kissing everyone. Those feelings of freedom and abundance. Living a life full of things that are so inconsequential. That is my idea of heaven.

Honor Blackman

Actor

3 January 2010

At 16, I was rather serious. I'd already started work as a clerk in the civil service which made me feel wondrously independent. I was astonishingly innocent compared to today's teenagers but quite happy. I had just started elocution lessons and I was very wrapped up in learning poetry and the theatre and I found that world very exciting.

My father slapped my face when I first put on lipstick. I was about 18. He had such high standards, one never quite measured up. He was the kind of person that when one was very small, one couldn't go for a walk and just enjoy the walk – one had to think of all the things that began with M along the way. You couldn't just enjoy life, there was always a price to pay. I was scared of him because he did give us clips around the ear or, on occasions, really whack us. I loved him – but then children do. Even if your father's a murderer you love him because you don't know any better and he's your father.

Letter to My Younger Self: Inspirational Women

My mother was full of reservations about my decision to go into the business. Actresses to her were the next thing to prostitutes. She didn't like it when I played bitches or unfaithful women. My father thought he could watch over me.

I had enormous trouble when I went to America to do the promotion tour for *Goldfinger*. Some interviewers wouldn't say the name of Pussy Galore. In fact they wouldn't allow *Goldfinger* into the States to begin with – it wasn't until the American press saw a picture of me with Prince Philip, headed 'The Prince and the Pussy', that they thought it would be alright. I don't think my father would have minded because I don't think he would have known a pussy was a name for a vulva.

My younger self wouldn't have believed you could make a life as an actress. I had a very stern teacher called Miss Hathaway who put me in a play when I was evacuated in the war. I met her later when I was in my first acting job and she said, 'You can't possibly imagine you'll be able to make a living doing that.' She must be dead now but I wonder how she felt later on when she found out it was perfectly possible for me to do just that.

Both of my children are adopted. I think it's important to let adopted children know they are adopted from as early as possible, otherwise you're lying to them. They are aware that they've been given away and the rejection is fierce. The teenage years can be very difficult. So woe betide you if you fail them.

I'd warn my young self that my father's voice will stay in my head long after he dies. The self-discipline thing stands to this day. I find it extra difficult to spend a weekend just reading for pleasure – I feel so guilty that I haven't done or learned more. I think my father made it hard for me to believe that anything I had was good enough, even husbands (Honor has been divorced twice). From someone so unsatisfactory herself, to have such high standards for other people is unforgivable but that's the way one was made.

Jacqueline Gold

Businesswoman
10 October 2011

Sixteen wasn't a great time for me if I›m honest. I lived with my mum, I was still at school and my home life wasn't good. My parents split when I was younger and my mother's boyfriend was abusive to me from the age of 12 to about 15. And to my sister too. So we lived in dread of him. I think I did feel some resentment towards my mother, but when you're a child and something like that happens to you, in some ways it feels like the norm. But it left me painfully shy and severely lacking in self-esteem.

My mother was very strict with us, we weren't allowed to do anything or have any freedom. My dad would come round once a week but it wasn't a friendly environment so he'd just sit there saying nothing and so would I. I had a part-time job as a waitress so I did have a tiny bit of independence. That little job was very important, it was my escape. I didn't want to act like a victim, I wanted to have financial freedom and control. I wasn't confident but I had some inner strength and I wasn't going to let my difficult childhood beat me. I left home when I was 18.

If I could go back and talk to that young girl, I'd tell her there is nothing to fear more than fear itself. I wish I'd known that as you get older you grow in confidence – that would have inspired me a lot then. But I would never have believed it was possible. I wish I had been more assertive and more engaging with people but I couldn't do it. Unfortunately, I was in a very negative environment; I felt I didn't have permission to be outgoing and gregarious.

I'd definitely tell my younger self, even when you're shaking with nerves, if you make yourself do something, confidence will come if you really know what you're doing. I was 21 and working at my dad's business (David Gold, who owns Ann Summers and Knickerbox). It was really just for experience, but I came up with the idea of an Ann Summers party plan. I was very excited about it but putting it to the board – seven men – was very nerve-wracking. Very few of them thought it was a good idea. I remember one board member saying to me, women aren't even interested in sex. But the more knockbacks I got, the more determined I became about pushing on. The party plan took £80,000 in the first year and grew at a rate of 20 per cent a year for many years.

Being recognised for my business contributions was a huge thing for me – probably the biggest moment of my life was meeting the Queen. Opening my first store in Dublin in 2004 was a memorable moment. There have been lots of challenges that I would never have thought myself capable of doing when I was 16. I feel very proud of what I've achieved and helped others to achieve.

Letter to My Younger Self: Inspirational Women

I have an empathy with people now that I didn't have when I was younger, simply because I hadn't the life experience then to understand them. Now I look back sometimes and think, should I have treated that person differently, now I can relate to what they were going through. At the same time, if I could go back I wouldn't be so easily intimidated. I remember a male member of staff telling me to F off and I didn't know how to handle it. Now I don't stand for any nonsense.

Gurinder Chadha

Director

22 February 2017

At 16, it was all about school, school, school. I didn't go out very much, and if I did it was with my family. I'd never eaten in a restaurant; I'd never eaten Chinese or Italian food – it wasn't part of my parents' culture to go out to eat (Chadha was born in Nairobi to Indian parents; the family moved to West London when she was two). I lived the simple life of a goodie two-shoes Indian girl. But I did refuse to wear Indian clothes. I didn't want people to think I was just another goodie two-shoes Indian girl. I knew I was much more than that. So there are pictures of me at weddings – all the women around me are in these fabulous Indian clothes and I'm in a bright blue three-piece polyester suit.

My parents and I reacted differently to the growth of the National Front and overtly racist politicians. They wanted to put their heads down and ignore it, put up and shut up. I wanted to stand up and scream 'This isn't right'. I remember going on the demonstration down Fleet Street for the children who died in the New Cross fire (a house fire in 1981 which claimed the lives of 13 young black people, and which was thought by many in the community to be started deliberately as a racist attack). It was a very rowdy demonstration, quite scary – people were screaming and shouting at each newspaper as we went past their building. There were lots of policemen and we came across an Indian policeman and suddenly these Indian girls started shouting at him in Punjabi, basically calling him a motherfucking spooner, sucking up to the establishment. I was shocked at that – he was a policeman doing his job, being attacked by the Asian community.

I was at the first Rock Against Racism concert. My parents really didn't want me to go so I told them I was going shopping. I was too scared to go to the demonstration so I went straight to the park in Hackney. The Clash were in the middle of their soundcheck when I got there, then it went very quiet. I waited about an hour on this big empty park then thought, well, no one's going to come. It was a nice idea, what a shame. But as I was walking out of the gates, I heard the weird sound of hundreds of whistles coming towards me. I stood on a wall and saw thousands of people – black, white, Asian – all marching together. That was a defining moment for me. To see these white English people marching alongside Asians, and black people, marching for people like me, marching against racism. It was very moving and really defined my teenage years.

I wasn't allowed to even think about boys. But… there was one. I used to get the bus to school and I was often carrying my tennis racquet. There was this boy who was often standing at the bus stop across the road and he used to pretend to serve me with an imaginary ball. Of course I pretended I wasn't interested in looking. He ended up working in the Dominican cinema, the Indian cinema, in Southall. I didn't really care for Bollywood films at that age but I remember getting quite excited about going to that cinema because he was there, serving hot samosas and warm coke. I never spoke to him. I wasn't allowed to. And that was the extent of my teenage romance.

If you told the teenage me what her life was going to be, oh my God, I would never have believed it. That I was destined to travel to so many countries, to make movies, to touch people all over the world with my stories! When I was a young girl, whenever we came into central London from Southall we'd go along the A14, past The Bridge Hotel. It was just this little hotel with little orange lamps in the fake lead windows. But whenever we went past I would always think, wow, that's a completely different world to mine. I will never be that person who stays in posh English hotels like that. I think about that little girl every time I go past The Bridge Hotel now. That sums it up. Now I've stayed in the most fabulous five-star hotels in the world. That little girl had never even eaten in a restaurant.

I think my sense of who I am, that hasn't changed. That's what has taken me through. It hasn't been easy being the sole woman Indian director in the film industry for many years. Getting my stories out there, having my voice heard. But I do it with tenacity and determination. And I think that came from that 16-year-old girl who, when she told her school careers adviser that she wanted to go to university, was met with the response, darling, really? I think you should apply for secretarial college. At that moment I knew she had me for someone else. I think I'm still showing people who think I'm one thing that I'm really something else.

I was in my twenties before I decided I wanted to work in cinema. (She began as a BBC journalist.) That was when I realised how powerful the camera was in defining who we are. And people like me were always at the edge of the frame, or completely absent from it. I wanted us to be at the centre of the frame. *Bend It Like Beckham* was really about me, my teenage years growing up with my parents. My advice to my younger self would be to be even more vociferous in fighting to create those opportunities for those communities. Because you deserve them, and they won't come to you. You have to go out and get them.

My only regret is that my father died before he saw my success. That really has shaped me enormously. I've talked about it a lot and worked very hard to get over it. I was very close to my dad. He struggled a lot in his life and he relished everything I did. But he never got to see my big success with *Bend It Like Beckham* and that's always been a sore point with me. When I decided I wanted to become a journalist, then a filmmaker, he was over the moon. Though he'd always wanted me to do the classic Indian thing, become a doctor, he really appreciated that I wanted to represent my community. His younger brothers are both here with me now. They saw my new film (*The Viceroy's House*, which deals with the Partition of India), and my uncle was very moved by it. He said I'd done a great job and my father would be very proud of me. That really meant a lot to me.

If I could go back to any time in my life, when I was at my absolute happiest, I'd go back to my first Christmas with my baby twins. When they were podgy, juicy little things you could squeeze and hold and carry around. I thought I was never going to have them (she and her husband spent years struggling with IVF) so to have them, to have two, a boy and a girl – that was just amazing for me.

Vicky Pryce

Economist and business consultant
20 October 2013

When I was 16 my main concern was leaving Greece and getting to the UK. When I was 12 my father took me to London to learn English. I remember walking down the King's Road, in the time of hot pants and everything else. It looked so amazing. I was so impressed by the freedom in this country. Greece was a very conservative place at this time and, under the Colonel (Geórgios Papadopoulos who ruled Greece as a military dictator between 1967 and 1973), not a happy place. I was brought up in a relatively conservative way. Boys like my brother got all the attention. When I saw London I thought, this is it, this is my place. So I moved there when I was 17.

I felt that as a woman, the UK had far more opportunities for me. Having said that, I think I was the first woman economist to be employed by the bank I joined (Williams & Glyns Bank Limited, now part of RBS) after university. If I met the 16-year-old Vicky now, I'd be impressed because she's about to take a leap into the unknown. I'd be shocked and very worried if my daughter had done that so young. It seems mad now, to go to another country at 17, knowing no one, having no connections and having no money.

I think the younger me would be impressed that I've achieved complete independence, I made it in a man's world. She would have worried that having five children would be very constraining in terms of my career. But I took very little time off work when I had my children and I didn't really change my life. Because I was so convinced that women need to be themselves and continue being themselves, even when they became wives and mothers. I had seen families destroyed by the man's misfortunes and I felt women had to be independent – financially and emotionally – to avoid that. Without financial independence you can be lost to somebody.

It was crazy of my younger self to think she'd never have children. What ultimately does sustain you is family and friends. That's what gets you through the hardest day, and it turns out to be more important than anything else. But you also have to be a strong individual. Of course bad things affect you but as a mother you have to let the people who care about you know you're okay. Once I felt my children knew I was okay, my anxieties dissipated. They could carry on with their own lives, even when I was in prison (Pryce and her then husband Lib Dem MP Chris Huhne both served nine weeks in prison in 2012 when Huhne pleaded guilty to perverting the cause of justice; Pryce took driving licence penalty points incurred by him).

Before everything happened to me I believed that maybe women had achieved something in society. Now I'm completely convinced that feminism hasn't got us very far at all. What was written about me before, during and after the court case … there are always men who will take a certain attitude about what women should do. But what was extraordinary to me was how many women took the same attitude. When I got to prison, there was a huge solidarity among the women. The big shock was the real lack of solidarity outside.

When you're in a marriage you work as a unit. What happened in my marriage however did make me question whether you can have trust in any relationship. But if you don't, life is hell. I've thought about what I should tell my children. It's not straightforward. You can't say, don't trust anyone in life. Because then life's not worth living.

I am definitely closer to my children than I ever was. That's not just happened within the last year, it's been going on since my marriage break-up. And I relied on them to handle everything while I was away. They were my source of strength and that was brilliant. They put things in proportion. Nothing, nothing matters more than children. I've seen people lose a child. That is devastating. I couldn't put up with that. I could put up with anything else.

Glenda Jackson

Actress and politician
27 June 2022

I was still at school when I was 16. Then I left and my first job was working in Boots, the chemist, and my wages went straight to my mother. I lived in Hoylake in the Wirral and the Boots in Kirby was just a bus ride away. I was a good student until I was about 14. Then I think I just got bored and I didn't do particularly well in my exams. It became a very popular thing for me to hide in the cupboard making irritating noises during English lessons, I think I probably went on doing that for a good while. I came up with the idea but then everyone joined in. My classmates pretended not to hear the noises. We were just being beastly to the teacher. I can't remember whether I was actually ever discovered.

Most of my time was spent reading and, if I could afford it, going to the cinema. I can't remember the names of the black-and-white films I went to see but I do remember the women in them. People like Bette Davis and Joan Crawford. I had no idea what I might do for a career but a friend of mine was with an amateur dramatics society and encouraged me to join it, which I did. One of the people who ran it said I should go in for acting, so I wrote to the only drama school I've heard of, which was RADA. After an audition they offered me a place, but I couldn't afford to go. Then one of my managers at Boots – I'm ashamed to say I've forgotten his name – wrote to Cheshire County Council telling them about the offer and they paid my fees. I can't see that happening these days.

My family were very distressed that I was going away. My aunt who lived just around the corner thought she'd never ever see me again. But for me every day was exciting. I made a friend who was Canadian, and I stayed in the same digs not only for the two years at drama school, but after I left drama school and got a job down in London.

When I left RADA the chief told me not to expect much work before I was 40 because I was essentially a character actress, and that seemed quite reasonable to me at the time. But when I left, I got work immediately. However, after working quite assiduously for about two years, I then didn't work in the theatre at all for another two years. That's the theatre for you. I didn't have much money, but a very small amount of money meant you still could live in London in those days.

I never got to a point when I didn't worry that I wouldn't work as an actor again. I always felt that the last performance of whatever I was doing would be the last time I'd ever work. It's a very overcrowded profession, and particularly overcrowded if you're a woman. Authors don't find women that interesting. It was nice to win an Oscar (for *Women in Love* in 1970, after which she won again for *A Touch of Class* in 1973). It's nice for a role to be appreciated. But it's the work that matters. Making *Women in Love* was amazing. It was the first time I worked with Ken Russell and he was absolutely remarkable. I've been very lucky with the directors I've worked with.

I think, looking back, the most life- and career-changing work I did was with Peter Brook (the legendary multi award-winning film and theatre director). He is probably the greatest director the world has ever seen. To actually work with him and within the Royal Shakespeare Company was just amazing. The marvellous thing is, the work was just so, not overwhelming, but he was constantly finding new ways and new ideas. He was extraordinary. The really great directors don't dictate – they wait to see what you're going to do. And then they sort of nudge you around.

I was always at the tail end of the group when I was young so I'd be amazed to find out that when I got older, people actually wanted to know me. To work with me. I don't think I was particularly confident then. And of course it was a different world. There was only a certain amount expected of you as a woman, especially a working-class woman.

An interest in politics in terms of how the country was changing was a common theme with many millions of young people like me growing up after the Second World War. The differences in the classes in this country had begun to fracture. And an awareness of that was part of the changes that came about in me. But it was many years later that I decided to get seriously involved.

What persuaded me to give up acting and go into politics was Margaret Thatcher (Glenda retired from acting and became the Labour MP for Hampstead and Highgate in 1992, joining the Labour front bench as shadow transport minister in July 1996). That was the extremity of everything I thought was the worst way for the country to go forward. I was very fortunate to be re-elected five times. And to occasionally be able to really help the people in my constituency. It's such a privilege to be a Member of Parliament, to be able to open those doors to help people if they need it.

Of course the House of Commons wasn't welcoming for women, but in my generation, we're so used to that. In a funny kind of way you'd be surprised if it wasn't immediately apparent. You expect to be ignored, so you have to be prepared for that. When I was elected in 1992 there were 35 female MPs, I think, and that was considered quite a lot. I gave my maiden speech to a virtually empty House, but that was okay. Of course it makes you angry but even that marks you up as 'woman, failure'.

It's not that I don't agree with what the modern women are saying or trying to do, but I think we are still in a society where what women say, think, do has to be scrutinised and pursued. Look at this whole argument about HRT (women going through the menopause are still frequently denied access to, or steered away from, what can be life-enhancing treatment). What older woman hasn't experienced that? Yet it's taken until the middle of the 21st century for Parliament to actually air it and talk about it. It's still the case that whatever men do is widely accepted, whereas when the media consider what women do, there's always an element in the reportage which is critical. I do think that culture is beginning to crack, but it's by no means equal yet.

If I could have one last get together with people I've lost over the years – well, I'd be hard pushed to pick just one of my family. I imagine they'd all be there and the conversation would mainly be them criticising me. And I'd be fine with that. As any working-class person knows, humour is a large part of how families communicate, but it also involves being immensely critical of you and all the neighbours and everyone else.

If I could live one moment of my life again it would be seeing my son for the first time. They knocked me out during my actual labour. When I came round I was in a hospital bed and they brought this baby in, and that was my son. That kind of responsibility can feel frightening, of course. But to see this tiny creature in my arms. Oh, it was amazing.

Chapter 6:

Family

Nancy Sinatra

Singer and actor

27 January 2021

I was a pretty upbeat, contented 16-year-old, I followed all the rules. I loved school. I excelled and I loved it. I didn't rebel at all. I wore straight skirts, and sweaters and saddle shoes and Bobby socks. The shorter skirts came later. Home life was pretty ordinary. I had a brother and a sister and a mother, and my dad would come and go. We were very, very close, all of us. In my high school years, my dad wasn't as famous or popular as he became later or as he had been prior, in the Big Band days in the '40s. It was all kind of normal.

I was into all kinds of music when I was a teenager. I composed a lot of music for the school concerts, which we had every year. And I used to go to the record stores all the time. There was one in Hollywood called Music City. There was another one called Sam Goodies, I think. You used to be able to take a record and play it in the store in the booth before you purchased it. And we had dance parties, when we'd put on records. I loved Harry Belafonte and my favourite in the early days was Johnny Mathis. I love him so much. He's a dear friend. He's a very kind, generous person.

I was so immersed in music that it was sort of a fait accompli that that's the way I would go in life. But it was pretty clear from the get-go that I'd have to work hard to get beyond my name. In the end I guess I got lucky. My choice of songs and things, that moved me out of the pattern. In the beginning I named myself Nancy Nice Lady because of the nature of the music I was doing, which was all bubblegum. And then later, Lee Hazlewood (the singer-songwriter and producer) came into my life and he nicknamed me Nasty Jones. He said I could be anybody and make hit records, I didn't have to be a Sinatra. I could be a Jones. He had faith in me and he gave me faith in myself. He gave me courage. So instead of bubblegum orchestral music, we went into a more country, funk kind of feel, which suited me much better. He really created that for me, and I'll be forever grateful.

As well as the way he recorded my voice, Lee surrounded me with great musicians. And we made music that was much more me as a person, that groovy funky rhythm section. There wasn't an opportunity to do that kind of thing before. When you work for a record label you do what the producer says. I was signed to Reprise but I don't think they wanted to sell me at all. I think I was only there because it was my dad's label. And they sort of had to tolerate me. I don't know, maybe I'm wrong, but I don't think I was that wanted there. My dad stayed out of it. He was very good about that. He knew that the best thing for me would be to be on my own, try by myself, and fall on my face if necessary.

I was manufactured. My look came from London, with

hair and make-up from New York. It evolved thanks to Mary Quant (the fashion designer) and a friend of mine named Amy Green. She took me to a salon called Kenneth in New York and I met a lady who coloured my hair blonde. And I loved that new persona. I was grateful for it because I had been floundering. It was playful and a little sexy. It was courageous for me to step out like that. I remember in Los Angeles when I was first wearing miniskirts, I would get smart alec comments like, are you going to play tennis today? People in LA didn't understand the fashion trend – it took people like Jean Shrimpton coming to America to really nail it.

I was pretty innocent, and kind of boring in my early twenties, I was quiet and dull. I didn't do the glamorous kind of life. The first advice I would give my younger self is not to get married so young. It was a stupid, stupid thing to do. That's number one. Don't do it. Continue your education, it enriches your life. I was married for a few years and then I was divorced. And then I was at sixes and sevens for a while, trying to figure all that out. I really should not have got married then. There was nothing wrong with Tommy (teen idol singer Tommy Sands), he was adorable, but we were just too young. But if you wanted to have sex in those days, and you were a quote 'nice' girl, you got married. Stupid.

My family was always very musical, going right back to my grandparents. I was very close to all four of my grandparents. My mother's parents passed away when I was in my early teens, but I had enough of them to have been encouraged by them and loved by them. My father's mother Dolly, she used to sing a lot and his father Marty used to sing too. They had a bar in their house where they would have singalong parties. There was music all the time. These days I don't listen to my own music very much to tell you the truth, but lately I've had to listen because of this new compilation of my songs. Do I hear anything of my father's voice in my own singing? You know, sometimes I do. Sometimes it comes back at me a little bit, every now and again.

If I could go back in time I would probably take more jobs that were offered me along the way. I was nervous and shy and I didn't take advantage of opportunities that I had. And that's very sad. They say that what you regret at the end of your life is not what you did, but what you didn't do. And there's a lot of stuff I didn't do. I was offered a TV series where I would have been a mom with a 14-year-old child. And I said something real smart alec, like I'm too young to have a 14-year-old child. No, thank you. In actuality, I was not too young but for some reason I had hurt feelings that they would offer me something like that. But I should have done it. I should have taken it.

I lacked a certain amount of confidence. I was okay with a certain amount of success but I didn't feel confident enough to really pursue a big career. I don't know why. I think I was just too shy. Maybe it wasn't the career for me. I've always been interested in anthropology. If I'd stayed in school, I might have gotten into that. But I also believe in destiny. And I think I was brought here to the planet to contribute something to women. And I hope I've done that.

If I could have one last conversation with anyone it would be with my mother. She was the wisest person I've ever known. I spent every day of the last weeks of her life at her house, bringing her items of comfort and food and just sitting with her, keeping her company. I guess I did what I could. But when she actually took her last breath, I wasn't in the room.

My sister was there. I had gone to the pharmacy to pick up medication for her and by the time I got back to the house, she was gone. I had said everything I wanted to her. Time and again. I just would like to have been holding her hand as she passed, but I wasn't.

There were a lot of wonderful days and weeks and months at the desert house (in the San Fernando Valley, California) when I was growing up. If I could relive any day from my life it would be then, around Christmas or Easter time at our family home. My brother and I playing either on the lawn or in the swimming pool. My mom pregnant with my sister, my dad sitting in the sun. I think it would be that day.

Samantha Morton

Actor and director
31 January 2019

At 16, I was living in a homeless hostel in Nottingham – it was called an independence unit but basically it was a dumping ground for kids who had to leave care. We were just forgotten about really, with no support or follow-up. The people who ran the unit were great, they were as helpful as they could be with helping you get your money or apply for college. But it was a very tough time. I felt a lot of anger when I was a teenager. I'd been in care since I was a baby, so it had been a massive part of my life. I was angry at the system, the state, for failing to take care of me in the most basic common sense way. Why was I being abused by residential social workers but I couldn't stay the night at my friend's house because their parents hadn't been checked out? Of course I was angry.

My stepfather, who I adored, was Glaswegian and very outgoing. If I'm anyone's child it's not my mother's or my father's, it's my stepfather's. I'm very like him – he was very outspoken and a real character. Despite my unstable upbringing, I was never shy. I loved fighting for the right to do or say something. I always had my hand up in class. And my stepfather supported me in everything I did. I lost touch with him for certain reasons. But when I was with him I did say thank you. He knew how grateful I was.

Sometimes all you need to turn a child's life around is one person who notices, who cares, who goes the extra mile. For me it was Mr Thompson at my junior school. He saw something in me. He knew I liked doing school plays and he encouraged me to visit the Central Junior Television Workshop run by Ian Smith. So I went to an audition and the rest is history. I found drama and I found Ian Smith. He became my teacher, my mentor. He was the guy I phoned when I was in the cells again. He was incredible to me. I was in and out of the Workshop from age 14 and when I was 16, and ready to really turn my life around, I got back in touch with him. I told him I wasn't into crime anymore and I'd cleaned up my act, having been part of the rave scene. He put me back into the Workshop, got me to auditions, and I started to get proper speaking parts. I owe so much to those two teachers.

If I hadn't found drama I still believe I'd have had an amazing life. It would probably have been in socialist politics or activism but I always had a feeling I was going to be alright. I was bright and determined. By 16 I had found an inner strength, I felt I'd sorted myself by then, I'd found a calm. People have a misconception about kids in care. They assume they have no love in their life. The state were no help to me but I did feel love and support from certain individuals who were trying to do their best for me. So I always had hope. That's what the film I made, *The Unloved* (released in 2009), was all about.

If I could go back in time and really impress the 16-year-old Sam, I'd tell her about the family she's going to have. Not the movies, the Oscar nominations – that world would seem shallow to young Sam. But she would be so excited to think that one day she'd have a family that she loved and loved her in return. If I really wanted to show her a great achievement, I'd show her Esmé, my first child. It was bloody hard work being a mum. And it was scary. Having had 12 foster parents, I didn't have any reference points for that consistent kind of family. But I loved it from the start. I have three children and I'm proud of all of them and I feel dead lucky.

When I had a daughter I didn't feel sad for my younger self. What I felt was angry at the lack of support for my mother when she was suffering. She was in a very abusive marriage and when she tried to find help with her children everybody turned her away. And she didn't know who to go to when she was running away. Now I think God, if I could go back and grab my mum and say, right, Pam, this is what you need to do. Here are the agencies who can help.

I think I've had some real close shaves. As a young unaccompanied actress going to auditions with strange people in strange places, being asked to do things that were not in the script but not feeling able to say no. I remember when I was in *Band of Gold* (mid-'90s ITV series), there was a scene a particular director wanted me to do topless, though that wasn't in the script. I was 16 years old. Sixteen! And I was having a sex scene with a man in his sixties. And I was sobbing in the trailer and it was all 'Sam's being tricky'. I didn't understand that I had a right to say I didn't feel comfortable. I felt I was from the streets and I'd won the lottery even being in the show, rather than feeling I had earned the right to be there. Some of the male directors working in TV drama in the '90s were delicate and kind. And some were bullies and brutal.

Once I started making films in America I'd started speaking out about the industry and lots of people just didn't employ me. If, for instance, I saw crew being overworked, not being properly paid, having accidents because they're so tired, I'd speak up against it. And lots of people don't like that, they don't like trouble causers. And there are plenty of people who are media trained and they go to work and they're just not themselves. They put on a smile and they play the game. But if you grow up in the care system then work in the film industry, which is basically an old boys' club... it used to put my back up quite a lot.

Sometimes I get very tired looking back at my teenage years; I felt like I'd lived a hundred lives before I was even 16. Now I don't like big drama in my life, I like it to be smooth. So for me the good thing that comes with age is peace inside. But with that peace is the fear of mortality. I think, I'm 41. If I'm lucky, I might get to 80. Oh, I've done half my life. I do for various reasons live each day as if it were my last. Which can be very intense. But I try to be in the moment as much as possible. I think I'm still very ambitious as I feel as an actress I get better as I get older. So I'm hungry for the big parts. But in my private life, I want to relax and enjoy it. I know what makes me happy now. And I feel lucky.

Mary Portas

Retail consultant and broadcaster
2 March 2015

When I turned 16 I was a carefree thing. I'd just done my O-levels and I remember that hot summer of 1976, lying down outside, listening to 10CC's 'I'm Not in Love' with my pals Carrie and Debbie, thinking about our futures and our freedom. And then my mum died and suddenly it was the end of my childhood. Quite firmly. It was even the end of my childhood character, this naughty girl, the leader of the gang. You can only be like that if you feel free and I didn't feel free anymore.

My mother was the matriarch. In that wonderful, capable way, she was the centre that we all orbited around. I think of that game swingball; you have this central base and you can bash the balls around because you know the centre is solid. In my book I write, 'How lucky was I to get you?' I truly believe my mother gave me my foundation, and she left my life when I was just about baked, ready to come out of the oven –

though really I believe you need your parents until you've fully transferred your love to someone else. She was able to darn, cook, do arithmetic with us, she played the violin. I just lucked out that I had her.

My life now is so extraordinarily different to the one I grew up in. Here I am, a gay woman, with a family. That deep-rooted Catholicism that was so central to my mother, I had to turn my back on that – so much of it is frankly ridiculous and limits people's ability to be. I don't really measure myself against her values. But I do often check in with her, have a chat with her in my head.

After my mother died, I cloaked myself in a protective air and probably gave out a little element of cynicism. That great Irish wit, that gift for the one-liner, that was a huge part of my character, but in my teens I moved towards fear and that gave me this anger that I had to suppress. My daughter now is on her gap year and I look back and think, Jesus, that kind of idea, that freedom, didn't come into my life. Because if I'd gone away, I'd have had nothing to go back to.

I think if I met the teenage Mary now I would know that this child was in pain. I would see a little terrier, yapping and biting, but with a heart underneath. Every terrier needs stroking and loving and that's what I would do if I met her now. I would tell her, listen, my darling, the world will look after you. The world is a kind and a good place. Please don't be fearful; try to find in yourself the core strength you have and we'll build on that. And I would tell her, creativity is the light, the fire in your life. Don't consider the path that will make you money, go down the path that will make your heart sing.

My life really took off in my early thirties. I remember it all clearly. I started working (as creative director) at Harvey

Nichols. I loved the place and the people so much, and I just started to fly. I'd just turned 30 and I started to make money. I loved what I was doing, I knew I could make a change, I had just got married and I was in love.

Every bit of my life now would surprise the teenage me. Except that I have children. I always wanted a family, family was so intrinsic to my thinking. I think the public profile would excite her. She always thought she would be a name, but she'd expect that to come from being an actress. I thought I'd be on the stage. Being recognised on the street – she'd have said yes, oh gosh yes, yes, yes to that. But she wouldn't have guessed she'd end up a businesswoman, with television shows, and with the wealth I've had.

The teenage me moaned all the time about being skinny. Now I'm so envious of her figure! Back then, I just didn't think my body was sexy. But I was 5'9", skinny. I could have worn anything if I'd had the confidence, but I didn't. All I wanted to do was put on weight. I remember Marc Bolan went to the States and came back a bit chubby, and I said, Mum, I have to go to the States. But we couldn't afford to go to Margate.

If people can't understand how I fell in love with men and am now married to a woman – well, that's their problem! I fell in love with both. I knew that could be the case early on, I had a big crush on Kate Jackson (from the '70s TV show *Charlie's Angels*) when I was young. I know plenty of people the same. We can't be boxed in – get over it. There are genuine shades of sexuality, that's the only way you can explain it. You meet someone and they just light something in you and you light something in them.

I think I've been a strong and good mother. That's the thing I'm most proud of. The only thing I would change is when my son Mylo was born – I went back to work at Harvey Nichols when he was three and a half months. I do regret that. This was 1994, it was a very different ballgame. I was the breadwinner. The stress and pressure overtook the time I should just have held him. All kids want is structure and love and sometimes you've just got to go with that because it all goes past so quickly.

I remember getting to 40 and thinking eek! Then I was 45 and thought how good it was being 40. Then I was 50, thinking how good 45 was. Now, at 53, I assume I'm going to look back one day and think wow, what I'd give to be 53. I've decided to just enjoy life. I spent too many years working too hard.

If I could back to a pivotal time in my life, it would be when Melanie and I took my kids, Mylo and Verity, to San Francisco. We met up with great friends who live out there, they have this great old beach house. I remember those evenings, walking on the beach and just knowing this was my new family unit and how special that was. It worked and it was beautiful. This was around 2004, before gay marriage, and there weren't many gay couples with kids. If I'd have known then that ten years later, we'd be where we are now... Wow, we've come far.

Mariella Frostrup

Journalist and broadcaster
10 May 2010

My dad died when I was 15 and that caused enormous trauma in my life. It resulted in me leaving Ireland where I'd been living with him and coming to London on my own. I was old before my time as a result of what had been quite a complicated childhood – my parents had divorced and I'd been to 11 different schools. I never had a chance of any kind of stability.

There had been a sense of existential despair at home with my father chain-smoking and drinking too much in one corner and my mum, who was a painter, painting these terrifying scenes in the basement of the house. But they loved us so much that they instilled in me a degree of confidence and a sense that I could do things with my life despite the obvious disadvantages I'd had.

I think the very formative thing that happens to you as a child is when you decide that you, as opposed to the adult parent, are better placed to take responsibility for yourself. It happens to us all at different points but it happened to me incredibly young, around 14. I think the lack of security made me determined to create something permanent, solid and tangible. I was terrified into working very hard.

If I met my young self now I'd think she was a bit peculiar. I was really serious about many things, I shouldered a degree of responsibility that was silly for a kid my age. I'd tell her to loosen up and live a little. I was very serious and fearful. I bought my first flat at 18. I was so sensible. Patsy Kensit (the actress, model and singer), one of my old clients when I worked in the music business, once said to me, you were just so intimidating, you used to wear suits and flat shoes and you were very glam in a very grown-up way – this was me at 19!

Like a lot of young girls I hero-worshipped my father and I've had to re-examine my feelings and my relationship with him in later life. To me he was an incredibly large presence, very inspiring and commanding intellectually. He wasn't that interested in children so you were always trying to up your game to interest him. That's also stayed with me. I recently met his best friend and he described him as a very inspirational character who had a big impact on his life, so I felt better that he'd loomed so large in mine. But he was also a very heavy drinker, that's what killed him in the end.

I'm in awe of some of the qualities I had when I was young. It took guts getting on a ferry penniless, going to London and chasing work in the music industry. Youth is always open with possibility so you need that kind of bravado. But if you look back on my life, in London in the music business in my twenties – hanging out with Frankie Goes to Hollywood (the '80s pop band) in LA, being wrapped up in a business sloshing with money, flying all over the world in great hotels, it could have been very hedonistic and wild but the private me was too worried about things like saving money. Every time I made a friend I'd dress like her for a week because I had no confidence in my own style. It's taken me about two decades to achieve any level of personal style.

I'm not envious of the way I felt about the world when I was younger. If you'd asked me if I wanted children I'd have point-blank said no, I felt the world was a terrible, frightening place. I was so vulnerable and desperate for stability I got married at 18. Like a lot of insecure people, on the one hand it's compelling to have the sort of recognition that fame brings, but I don't think it does anything to assuage your insecurity. The fact that I hadn't finished school, despite being an academic child – and the fact I was a woman – made it hard for me to be taken seriously. I've been the music biz blonde. Then I was the film blonde. Now I'm the book blonde. The only constant has been the incessant reference to my hair.

I've never been happier than I am now. Now I'm wrinklier and considered mature I'm allowed to exercise my brain power in a way I struggled to get the opportunity to do in the past. But I still resent the double time it took.

The 16-year-old me might feel my life has been an abject betrayal of her principles. I was nihilistic about everything. Now I'm happily married with children I've become a much more optimistic person. I'd tell my younger self that having children is the happiest and most fulfilling thing I've ever done. I almost get teary thinking about what my life would have been like without them.

Coleen Nolan

Singer and television personality
10 September 2018

I was touring with my sisters when I was 16. It was probably the height of our career. Touring the world, Japan, Russia, Australia, everywhere. It was a very full-on time. But I'd been performing with my family since I was two so it wasn't an unusual way of life for me. And I was with my family so it felt very safe. I was – I am – a real homebody and I spent a lot of time just wishing I was back home. I probably appreciate that time in my life now more than I did when I was going through it. I look back now and think wow, that was actually an amazing time in my life.

The hits started drying up in my mid-twenties. We were still working but we weren't really touring anymore. We were doing summer seasons and clubs. And then I met Shane (the actor Shane Richie to whom she was married from 1990 to 1999) and had my two boys and suddenly I thought, I'm not enjoying this anymore. We were going on stage at half one in the morning to people who were pissed. And I thought, I've left my kids at home to do this? People see the glamour of that kind of life, but they don't see that it's really, really hard work. You struggle to have any kind of normality. I didn't want to drag my own kids around, I wanted them to have the childhood I'd never had.

When I found out Shane had been unfaithful, I thought it was a blip and we'd have counselling and everything would be fine. If I could go back, I'd leave straight after the second affair. I stayed two years too long. But I was massively in love with him. To me, there was nothing missing in our relationship. He's said that too, he said he doesn't really understand what happened. Well, he does… he wanted to have his cake and eat it. I loved him but in the end I thought, I'm not one of those women who keeps turning a blind eye. I don't deserve to be treated like this. And I don't think this is a great way to bring up my children, thinking that this stuff is okay. In the end, I think we've done okay. We stayed really good friends and we still are.

My sisters still find it hilarious that I do a chat show (ITV's *Loose Women*) every day when I wouldn't say boo to a goose when we were younger. It wasn't a planned career move. I went onto a talk show to talk about my breakup with Shane, and it eventually became a regular job. And I loved it. I realised I did have a voice and things to say, I'd just never had a chance in that massive family. It was the first time in my life I felt truly independent, my own person.

I grew up just worshipping '70s boyband The Osmonds. If you'd told the 16-year-old me I'd end up meeting them so many times they became friends… wow. We chat away about how similar our lives were, touring with our families. But every now and again in the middle of the conversation I suddenly think, my God, this is The Osmonds, I used to cry over them! I'm always starstruck by famous people. If I'm on a red carpet I'm always looking around saying, oh my God, look who it is!

If I could have one more conversation with anyone, it would be my mum and dad. Because when they both passed I hadn't been doing *Loose Women* (the daytime panel chatshow on which she was a regular presenter) for long. I probably went through a phase when Shane and I broke up when I was struggling a bit. I was a single, full-time mum. That must have worried them. I've done so many amazing things since they passed. I'd like to go back and tell them, you know, I'm going to be alright.

I think as a parent, and I hate to be sexist, but definitely as a mother, I don't think there's a moment after they're born when you don't feel guilty about something. Even now – Shane Jnr is 30 this year and I still worry and I still feel guilty. I do ask them, do you think when you're older you'll look back and think, I wish my mum hadn't done that? Bless them, they've always said no. But I'm sure there will be some things. I tried to protect my boys during the divorce. I made sure they never heard me and their dad rowing. I never ever used them as weapons, though that would have been the easiest way to hurt Shane. But I knew it would only hurt the boys. I'm very lucky, they've turned out to be really lovely boys. But they'll always be from a broken home.

I don't ever try to make my kids feel guilty for growing up, but I tell you what, I do sometimes have this urge to lock all the doors so they can't leave. Obviously at certain ages there are times you want them to just grow up and sod off. But that passes. I'm lucky we've got such a close relationship and we're such a big part of each others' lives. And they're very affectionate, they're good at giving me hugs. But I can't control them anymore, I can't ground them or tell them what to do. You do have a moment when you suddenly think, right, that's it, my job is done. That's all I was here for. So what do I do now? And that's quite shocking.

For the last three years of my marriage with Ray (the guitarist Ray Fensome to whom she was married from 2007 to 2018) we did everything we could to save it. And yeah, we could have said, I'm in my fifties, you're in your sixties, we're too old to start again. Let's just stay together and carry on. Because we weren't rowing or anything. We were just leading separate lives. I just decided, I don't want to just settle and I don't want a lodger. So I'd rather you just leave and we can be great friends. And that's worked out really well. I don't look back at the last 17 years as a failure. I look at them as being really great and giving us Keira, our fantastic daughter. I'm much happier, now that the decision has been made. But I do sometimes feel absolutely overwhelmed with sadness. Because when I married him he was the love of my life and we were going to be together forever.

If I could go back to any moment in my life it would be when I was in my mid-thirties. I'd broken up with Shane and I had thought I'd never be in love again, I'd never have any more children. Then there I was, in love and pregnant. It was such a happy 'world is my oyster' time. I loved my thirties, and my forties. I'm not really loving my fifties. I think partly because I lost my sister – that really makes you question your own mortality. And my kids are growing up, and now there's my second marriage gone. And I'm thinking, oh Christ, here I go again.

Chapter 7:

Friendship

Jennifer Saunders

Actor and screenwriter
19 November 2013

At 16, I was mainly preoccupied with horses. I didn't do a lot of school socialising, I had my horse friends and my horses, and I was quite happy. I went down to the local riding school; I didn't even have the gear, I just had my wellies, but I longed to go there because you could have a particular relationship with one pony. And things like Champion the Wonder Horse were on TV so you could live inside this fantasy the whole time. I still do, isn't it tragic?!

I moved around a lot as a younger child, due to my dad's job (a pilot in the Royal Air Force) but by 16 I'd been to the same school for a while. I was okay at school, and okay at most things. I didn't excel at much really, not even riding, but I still loved it. I was quite happy in my own head, as long as I had enough alone time, to go for walks or just think. I'm still the same. I think I'd go a bit mad if I couldn't be alone quite a lot.

Letter to My Younger Self: Inspirational Women

I always had body issues, anxieties, even when I was at my thinnest. I did a lot of exercise but I had this constant, I'm too fat, I need to go on a diet, I wish I was thinner. I thought a lot about what I would eat that day. Honestly, it makes me ill when I look back at photographs of myself at that age because I think, God, look at you! There's nothing of you! You worried about being fat and having spots – you've got three spots, you're 9 stone; get over it!

We were a very secure family. I think that came from moving around a lot, we stayed tightly in our family unit. It didn't matter where we went as long as we all went together. When I was writing my book I found loads of old letters written by school friends from places I'd just left, filling me in on what had happened since I left. It was rather nice.

If I met the teenage Jennifer now I'd think she was a bit angry. People did often say that, even when I'd didn't feel angry; maybe my face just falls into an unfortunate resting position. I think I'd have to do some work trying to get through to her before I knew anything about her. But we'd share an enjoyment of analysing people, people-watching, trying to always find the funniest thing in any situation. We could watch TV together, being very critical, always looking for the funny. I grew up doing that. Morecombe and Wise, Dick Emery, always Tommy Cooper, and Lucille Ball was a huge influence. She was such a great clown and I loved that.

If you told the teenage Jennifer she was going to be a performer rather than just a writer, she'd be very surprised. And she'd be surprised that I'm quite confident now. She'd love the success and the high profile, it would be a dream come true. She'd love the idea of being famous. I don't have any memory of being any kind of performer in my teens but I think my memory might be a bit faulty. I thought I was a bit grumpy and anti-social but my school reports say I was quite jolly and good-humoured. I didn't do any performing but in our family you always had to be able to make people laugh with a good story. I remember doing impressions of school teachers and getting caught by a teacher doing an impression of her in front of the class.

The younger me would be very pleased that I've managed to keep family life and career life both going. That I have a happy relationship I've managed to keep going. I still feel quite proud of that. She'd be equally impressed that I met Mickey Finn from T-Rex. That would be huge for her. And the fact that I'm now a show-jumping ambassador and I've met lots of top show-jumpers. People like Harvey Smith and Marion Coakes, one of the biggest heroines of my life. I would have died to have met her at 16.

When I first met Dawn (comedy partner Dawn French) I wasn't keen on her. Would I give her more of a chance if I could go back? No, no, no! These things take time, sometimes lots of time. You have to just be true to who you are. I might advise my younger self to make more of an effort though. In fact, I think I could say that generally. I could be quite lazy. Things often turn out to be more interesting than you first thought if you just make an effort.

I think when I had breast cancer I handled it quite well. I talked to people. I have amazing friends. They were all fantastic. It's only the chemo you have to go through. The rest of it I could cope with. If you think of it just as a really tough medicine you have to take for a while, it's all quite manageable. Though I'd tell my younger self to eat more healthily.

Personally, in terms of my work, I'm probably most proud

of *Ab Fab*. Because I did that on my own. I didn't have any expectations about it so when I think about it I think, yeah, I am actually really proud. It came just as this mad celebrity culture was about to explode, people were getting into fashion. It did feel like a different time. I wasn't really in that culture but I knew people in it and I could see people in it and it did seem to make sense.

I think my best, happiest times are when I'm just with the family. The absolute best times are when we're all together, on holiday, on the Amalfi coast, eating a beautiful meal and drinking wine. Those are my absolute, perfect days.

One of the most exciting days of my life was when Dawn and I saw our names in the listings of *Time Out* magazine. Dawn brought the magazine round to my house in Chelsea. She kept saying, 'Look, look, look' and more than anything else I remember that moment, when we actually saw the words 'French and Saunders' in tiny print. We just kept looking and looking at it, then we cut it out and stuck it in a scrapbook. It was proof, we were a French and Saunders. We'd made it.

Mel Giedroyc

Comedian and TV presenter
19 November 2012

Picture the scene. It's 1984. I'm 16. I was obsessed with those surplus military shops so I was in monkey boots and these huge white Guantanamo-style overalls with the crotch swinging at your knees and a massive baggy arse. And I had very short spiky hair, a T-bar of spots on my face, and wore very pale foundation. Not attractive. But my best friend, Sid, was gorgeous. I didn't have a bloody chance with boys being her best friend, so I was there, I think, to provide a bit of entertainment. I did cop a few snogs but I was more interested in just being with my mates.

I had such a good time as a teenager but now I'm in total fear that my own daughters will do all the things I did. I was the last of four kids and I had pretty much total freedom. There's tons of stuff my parents don't know about. It's only now that I'm in my mid-forties that I'm starting to tell them things, and they're sort of laughing. But their eyes are twitching. I think, hopefully, my daughters are much more mature than I am. Even now, and they're eight and ten. I mean, I just piss about for a living. I was in a pantomime, for God's sake.

If I met my 16-year-old self now, with my older cynical head on, I'd say, 'Why are you trying to be friends with everyone? Calm down.' But I'd love to tell her about this great friend she'll meet at university (Mel's comedy partner Sue Perkins). In the middle of this male-dominated comedy scene she'll meet this kindred spirit who laughs at all the same things as her. And five years later they'll make their debut at the Edinburgh Fringe, in a 10am comedy show called *The Naked Brunch*, and though their average audience will be around one person, they will love every minute.

During my twenties I got very angsty and broody. My brothers and sisters started having loads of babies and I got into my late twenties and started panicking; oh my God, it's never going to happen to me. I'd take my younger self aside and say, you're going to be a bit of an old bird when you have your first child – you'll be 33 – but don't ruddy worry about it. And don't worry about meeting someone. You get to meet him when you're 31, he's really nice, he's called Ben, it's all cool.

My kids are the best thing that ever happened to me. I know that sounds flipping cheesy but it's totally true. They just blew me away. They make everything worthwhile. They're so much fun and so interesting. It's such a bloody privilege. I remember looking at my first baby, just a few days old in her little basket, and I was suddenly very aware of my own mortality. I'd never thought about dying before. It's a weird one. It signalled my sudden going back to church – that fear of death, it made me go back to praying.

If you'd told me I'd get a BAFTA for *The Great British*

Bake-off I would literally have laughed in your face. Sue and I took that gig thinking, here we go, another cooking show among thousands of cookery shows. We enjoyed making it, nice people, loved the bakers, blah blah. But oh my God, it was amazing. It's ridiculous that we got paid to do it because Sue and I just had a laugh and ate loads of delicious cakes.

I'd love to go back to being 16, when my mum bought me and my sister tickets for this sketch comedy show. I remember sitting there – it was like the sun breaking through the clouds, a real road to Damascus moment, choirs in my head. I just thought, this is it, what I've been searching for. An incredible moment.

Julia Donaldson

Writer
20 April 2020

I was quite an immature teenager, not worldly wise, even though I grew up London in the Swinging Sixties. I wasn't an angsty teenager, I was intelligent and quite competitive, the kind of person who always came top in English. I went to an all-girls school so I didn't have a boyfriend though I'd sometimes go to parties and try to wriggle out of the clutches of boys who just wanted a quick snog. I did have a huge crush on Mick Jagger. I preferred the Beatles' music but Mick Jagger was sexier. I kept a teenage diary and there's lots about him in it. My friend and I would find clever ploys to try to get to meet him. I remember once we hung outside the Stones' concert and I tried to convince the security guard I'd met Mick Jagger in a park in Hampstead and he'd lent me an LP. I persuaded them to take a note to his dressing room and they came back and said, he does remember you but he's just about to go on stage so he can't chat now. I was a very naive girl.

I was quite close to both my parents and even more to my sister. There was also my aunt and uncle and my grandmother – we lived in the same house but on different floors. We would meet up for Sunday lunch and play Monopoly with my aunt and uncle. My father had polio, he was in a wheelchair. And so it was nice, looking back, that we had other adults around who could get involved in a more physical kind of activity. My parents were very, very good parents. They weren't at all meddling, interfering or pushy. Mostly they just let my sister and I get on with it. We'd go walking through Hampstead Heath, and across the city – we were quite lively, and had a kind of freedom parents these days might not allow.

I didn't want to be a writer at first, I wanted to be an actress, I was very stagestruck because when I was a bit younger I'd understudied the fairies in *A Midsummer Night's Dream* at the Old Vic in a star-studded production. So I could spout iambic pentameters, which must be where my flair for metre and rhythm comes from. That was my ambition, to go to drama school. I wasn't very glamorous but I was interested in clothes, I wasn't frumpy. I was quite inspired by the actresses in that production of *A Midsummer Night's Dream*, Judi Dench and Barbara Leigh-Hunt.

I gave up my acting ambitions quite gradually. I didn't get into drama school so I applied to university instead. After I graduated I was very much with Malcolm (her husband, a doctor who became her regular musical partner) and I didn't want to go travelling round the country trying to get into rep companies. So I did kind of abandon my acting ambitions. But all of that spirit got channelled into performing because when I met Malcolm we went busking together a lot, and then we started performing in folk clubs and festivals. It's very satisfying because performance has largely come back into my life again. Although I'm regarded primarily as a writer, I probably spend more of my time devising shows based on the books. And although I'm not acting Lady Macbeth or anything like that, I am actually on the stage playing to thousands of people. I think my teenage self would be quite impressed with that.

What would surprise the younger me most would probably be that I ended up being best known for writing children's books. I'd probably be disappointed with that because I'd rather have become Helen Mirren. I wasn't an especially maternal person. My sister and I would take the neighbouring little children to the zoo sometimes and when I was in my 20s I ran a drama workshop for five-to eight-year-olds so I've had quite a bit of experience with children. But I knew I didn't want to rush into having my own. I wanted to enjoy my freedom. My sister had children very young and I could see how much they changed your life. I wrote a lot of songs for adults when we sang in the clubs but there was more of a market for the children's songs, that's what I could make money from, so that's how it all evolved.

Malcolm and I met through his university roommate and went busking together. When my girlfriend and I were in Paris studying he came over and we went busking there too. So we were absolute bosom buddies. But it wasn't till I was back in Bristol when it developed into a real romance. Which was lovely. I think I would tell my teenage self, don't go running after Mick Jagger, it's actually much more satisfying and exciting to have a romance with someone you already know. You don't have to pretend you're something you're not. He's always been a part of my shows and he comes on all the foreign tours. We've played all around the world, Australia, Bermuda, China, Korea, Singapore, South Africa.

The Gruffalo sat on another publisher's desk for years. During that time, I'd go to schools and read the story and ask them to draw pictures of what they thought The Gruffalo would look like. One looked like an alien, one looked like a robot, but they all had purple prickles and everything else I mention in the story. Then Axel (Scheffler) came along and he did a few sketches. One looked like a wild boar, one a bit too much like an ogre. But one of them I saw and I knew very, very quickly that was my Gruffalo and now I just couldn't imagine him any other way. Axel has added so much humour and characterisation to my stories. I am eternally grateful to him.

It wouldn't be true to say that children's writers must all love all children. But I think it's true of me and maybe of a lot of children's writers that I do feel close to my childhood soul. I don't feel a huge gulf from the child or teenager I was. Some people feel, oh my God, how could I have been like that? But I don't. I don't love all children but I do absolutely adore my grandchildren and I'm finding it really hard now with lockdown. I have four girls and four boys, and they're still quite young. I was excited to see them after getting back from a tour in Australia, and now I still can't see them. I can't have a cuddle or tell them a bedside story.

If I could have one last conversation it would be with my parents. I wish my father had talked more about being in a German prisoner-of-war camp for five years. And I wish I could talk to my mother about her mother because my grandmother was a fascinating, captivating woman. She had this affair with Neville Cardus, who was a very famous *Guardian* cricket and music writer. And I think she played the piano like I play the piano and wrote some children's stories which weren't published. I'd love to quiz my mother all about her. But it's just too late now.

If I could go back and relive one time in my life it would be in Paris in 1969. I'd been busking with my girlfriend – we could only play a few chords on the guitar but we had dulcet voices and we always did quite well on the Champs-Élysées. Then suddenly Malcolm, who was just a friend then, arrived and that evening, we went out busking in the Place de la Contrescarpe in the Latin Quarter. And I just remember crowds gathering around and suddenly he was singing all these beautiful songs by The Who and from the shows. It was such an exciting, exhilarating moment, and we were still so young, not even yet in our prime. I think the best moments in your life are when you're totally in that moment, not wondering about what you'll think of that moment years later. And that was absolutely one of those.

Arabella Weir

Comedian and writer

20 September 2010

I was very popular with girls when I was 16. I had a very close gang of friends at my all-girls school which was incredibly reassuring – my friendships, I realise now, have been the most important things in my life before I had children. But I was over-concerned with my body weight. I knew I was a different shape to most of my friends and I had no information about why. I still remember my school nickname – banana tits. My breasts hung down right from when they started to grow, they grew droopy. I couldn't bear that, and I was obsessed with no one ever seeing them.

I became obsessed with getting boys to like me and by 16, my boyfriend actually lived with me. It was completely crazy, my mother should have said 'absolutely not' but she hadn't been parented properly herself. She was making it all up as she went along. I just told her I needed to be with him all the time, I was over-concerned about being loved by him, though I was still quite a stroppy, mouthy girlfriend. We were mad about each other. We were together for four years until he became a heroin addict. By then I was at university and I knew I'd been stupid, virtually a married woman at 20. But it was still heartbreaking when it finished, and I still struggle with things ending.

I had a combative relationship with my mother. I overindulged my dad – he lived in New York and I saw him so rarely that I was afraid to argue with him. So my mum, who stayed with her children, got all the shit as well as all the drudgery. She got a lot wrong but she had no idea what she was doing. She'd be all 'I love you so much', then 'I hate you'. She was like a lover. I gave her a tough time, 60 per cent of which she deserved, I think. But we also had some nice times. I'd like to go back and tell my teenage self, being a mother is harder than you know, you'll never know until you're a mother yourself. She's doing the best she can.

If I met the young Arabella now I don't think I'd like her. If I met her at a party with all her mates I'd think she was pretty ghastly. I seemed and wanted to seem very confident, because I wasn't. I was pretending all the time, talking all the time, always joking, never letting other people get a word in edgeways. I would just want her to be quiet.

I wish I'd joined many more drama groups – I was so concerned about hanging out with my cool mates. If you're interested in something you should learn everything you can about it when you're a kid. Don't worry if it's cool or not. I didn't do any of that. And I wish I could tell myself it doesn't matter what you look like – the confidence I could have had if I'd believed that for one minute. Then again, if I'd been very slim and got Greta Scacchi-type parts then, where would I be now? An out-of-work actress in her 50s.

Arabella Weir

The happiest I've ever been in work was when I was doing *The Fast Show* (a TV sketch show that aired from 1994). We had such a great time. I never felt that I shouldn't be here or worried they would find out I was actually a bit crap. For the first time ever, I thought I was exactly where I belonged. I put every fibre of my effort into doing that show and loved every minute.

I became a mother late and I'm incredibly aware of how lucky I am. I've made the most of it. I've worked out that confidence is key, but I also think it's important to admit when you've made a mistake and apologise for shouting or crossing a line. I want them to know everyone makes mistakes. That's why I hate celebrity magazines – the idea that anyone is infallible is dangerous.

The 16-year-old me would be astounded to find out I'd been successful. I tried hard to be popular in my gang of girls but it never occurred to me I'd have a successful career. Finding out what you want to do is the most important thing you can do as a young person. And I've made a life out of arsing around. How wonderful.

Andi Osho

Comedian and actor
8 January 2021

I was a bonafide geek at school, though I wouldn't have thought that at the time. I didn't feel like I fitted into the normal run of how everybody else was, so I found my tribe in the school choir. By the time I got to 16, I just couldn't wait to leave school. I wanted to get to college, because I was just done with it, I just completely had enough.

My mum and I had quite a tense relationship. Age 16 was so different for her because she'd grown up in quite a strict environment (in Nigeria). Her parents died when she was young, so she lived with an aunt and uncle who'd kind of fostered her long term. They weren't the greatest guardians, so I think that different experience for her made it difficult to deal with a 16-year-old who had been brought up basically British. We went head-to-head over a few things, like me wanting to go to Bros concerts (an '80s boyband), things like that. I think looking back she was very gracious, because she could have turned that on us, 'Do you know what I had to grow up with?' But she never did, she just had this kind of knowing silence and let things play out.

I didn't really notice as a 16-year-old that my mum has quite a cheeky sense of humour. It wasn't until I got older and I was just sitting talking with her that I realised just how much of a mimic she was, always going into people's voices from TV and making sarcastic asides. I was doing that from age 16 but it took me years to realise it came from my mother.

My being a performer didn't really come to the fore until I was in my 30s. I think my mum had this fear, what are you gonna do if it doesn't work out? She was really tense about it, and she was hurting, though she never really expressed it. Then when she started to see me regularly on TV I think she relaxed a little bit. If I could go back I'd tell my younger self to try to understand her better but the teenage me wouldn't listen because she was very impatient, and she was thinking about herself. It's not a good combination for listening to other people.

If you met me as a teenager you'd think, this person has too much energy for one human being. I was just a big, massive ball of energy. Even probably into my 20s I had too much energy and I didn't know what to do with it. So I put it into everything. I used to run everywhere. I don't even know when that stopped, I was incapable of just walking anywhere. And I just wanted to get into everything and do extra-curricular stuff at school. I started a newsletter. I even tried to start a pyramid scheme, telling everyone we were all going to make loads of money, until I got pulled in by a teacher and had it explained how it actually worked. And I was like, oh, okay.

I started as an actor and I got to a stage when I felt like

things had stalled. So I looked at all these actresses that I really liked, and they had all done stand-up or comedy sketches at some point in their career. That was really the motivation for me to say to myself, well, look what they've got. I could create something like that for myself as well. I remember doing a routine that I'd written for some people in my choir. It was mainly about our teacher, and our choir mistress, our school. And I'm not gonna lie, it went really well. So when I did it in adulthood, I felt very at home, just like that first time. I mean, it was still terrifying. I remember not even being able to speak at one point beforehand, I was so nervous. I didn't tell my friends in case it was awful and no one laughed. But when I actually did it, it felt like, yeah, I could do this, I could give this a go.

My big moment was getting on the comedy panel show *Mock the Week*. I had been kind of scrambling around the periphery, doing TV and plays, getting little breaks here and there. But the moment *Mock the Week* took a chance with me, it felt like that was the endorsement that other TV shows needed to take me seriously. It didn't happen immediately but that's what led me to doing other mainstream comedy shows like *Never Mind the Buzzcocks*, *Stand Up for the Week*, and *Michael McIntyre's Roadshow*. If I told the younger me she's going to do stand-up one day she'd just think that was ridiculous. Doing great dramas, that was part of my ambition, but the stand-up was kind of left field. And writing a book as well, that would surprise her (her novel *Asking for a Friend* was published in 2021). It's something I've wanted to do since I was really young. I wrote lots of little stories at school then tried to write a book when I was maybe 11. And I realised, gosh, this is really hard. And I just abandoned it. I think a younger version of me would just be like, you started writing a book? And you finished it? Are you kidding?

I think I'd tell my younger self to use all that energy in a good way – there were times it came out when I was cross. Looking back, what I'd really love to say to my younger self is, the sooner you can get your relationship with money sorted out the better. As soon as you can afford it, get yourself into therapy. As soon as you can, start reading books about relationships.

If I could have one last conversation with anyone it would be with my friend who died about ten years ago. Her birthday was late December and she would always have a little get together at the end of the year. And because Christmas had just happened I was always a bit like, I want to go but I'm so tired after Christmas. She died just after her birthday. I think if I was to go back, it would just be to go to that one birthday she had before she died. She used to laugh all the time, though she didn't have the same kind of sense of humour as me at all; she'd have been perfectly placed in a *Carry On* film. We also liked to have really interesting conversations about how the world is and how the world works. She was a bizarre combination because she loved her innuendos but she would also have really profound things to say about the human existential experience. So it would be lovely to sit down with her again. A little bit of innuendo and existentialism would be good.

If I could go back to any time in my life it would be that moment before I stepped on stage for my first night at the Hammersmith Apollo. That was really cool. I remember the steam from the smoke machine rising as I got ready to walk on stage, like something out of a singing show like *Stars in Their*

Eyes. At that point your mind can't go anywhere else. For me anyway, I cannot hold a single thought about anything else. I'm so, so present. I'm sure that night at the Apollo my heart was going mad but my mind just completely cleared. Because it had to, so I could go and do my job. And in that very quiet, special moment just before I went out, I kind of said to myself, blimey, mate. You did it.

Chapter 8:

Motherhood

Baroness Joan Bakewell

Journalist and TV presenter
12 March 2009

I was a conventional gymslip schoolgirl, in stockings and suspenders. At 16, I think I had just had my plaits cut off – they used to go down to my waist. I had rather unruly fine hair that wouldn't do the glamorous things I wanted and I was a bit chubby. I lacked confidence, though on the surface I think I was quite assertive.

I had very happy early years. I remember my parents' laughter very clearly. But when I got into my teens my mother began to suffer bouts of depression and that brought great conflict for me – this mother who'd been so joyous and full of laughter was suddenly not speaking to me. I thought it was my fault and I was constantly trying to placate her. It made me wary of people's emotions, rather thoughtful about them.

It was important that I had a rich interior life – I kept a lot of things to myself because I didn't want to risk being hurt.

My father I adored and he adored me – that might have been the reason for my mother's depression; I was clearly the favourite daughter. He was a businessman who had risen up from the foundry floor to become managing director of a small engineering firm. No one in my family had been to university and he backed me all the way to go and watched over my studies, made sure I did my homework.

I thought about the opposite sex all the time at 16. It was all very confusing because we weren't told anything. We went to the movies and I was enraptured by the high romance of films of the '40s and '50s, that was very important. I was completely enthralled by the Brontës, who of course had a weird idea of sex, which they didn't experience very much. Some day your prince will come is the most dangerous song ever sung in a movie because you can't hang around waiting for Mr Perfect, he's not there. At the time Mr Rochester would have been my prince, looking a bit like James Mason, he was very handsome with a wonderful voice.

I'd tell my young self that humanity is very varied. Just because there's a bit of trouble in your own family there's another world out there of people with entirely different temperaments, and having a depressive mother doesn't mean that anyone you ever love or who loves you will be the same. People have open minds and open hearts – that's the good news.

You have to be realistic about life and then you'll find it easier to get on. Don't have romantic illusions. I was part of a generation who taught its girls to be good wives, which involved waiting on their husbands all the day long, cooking, doing the shopping and laundry. I played that role in both of my marriages – it came naturally, it was part of the society from which I came in the '50s and '60s. Even when we were trying to be liberated in the '70s, we were trying to do everything, be a good wife and mother and do a job – it was quite tricky. My advice now would be, make sure your boyfriend can cook.

I would tell my younger self to wait until her thirties to have children. I had my first daughter when I was 25, the second when I was 29. Waiting longer would have given me a spell of adulthood in which I could you grow in confidence so when I came to have children I'd have had enough maturity not to be such a control freak. I was quite a controlling mother, trying to hold the fort all the time. If I'd had more of a career before the children were born I might have had more confidence. I wore out two copies of Dr Spock's baby book, I didn't know what to do at all. I was very anxious and felt a huge burden of responsibility. I thought 'this life depends on me'. But the good news is that children grow up anyway. I'd say now, don't be an anxious mother, you can convey that to your child – relax and enjoy them more. I didn't do that enough.

I had no career pattern – I seized the day. There are opportunities around you all the time, you've got to recognise them and grab them. I wish I'd written a novel earlier in my life. I got so much pleasure from writing it, even though I think I could be better. My advice would be to do the things you've always wanted to do before it's too late.

I'd also say to young Joan, don't be afraid of getting old. Stay healthy and enjoy it. Plan to live until you're 90 and don't regard everyone over 70 as a waste of time – they're not. At 16, I couldn't have guessed my life was going to be so good. People in those days found life quite humdrum and all the expectations were that mine would be too. It's been anything but.

Judy Murray

Tennis coach
3 July 2017

I was in my last year in school at a girls' school in Crieff. There was no high school in Dunblane then so my parents decided to send me to this private school in Crieff. I'll always be grateful to them for that because the sporting opportunities there were huge and obviously sport has been a massive part of my life ever since. I played netball, hockey, swimming, badminton and my life revolved around sport. My plan was to get accepted for university then take a year off to concentrate on tennis. All through high school I thought I'd be a PE teacher. But in fifth year I was advised away from that, there was a bit of scaremongering due to the precarious nature of that job at the time. So I ended up studying languages at university, which came in handy training the new tennis players coming through when I was coaching for the LTA (Lawn Tennis Association). (She is now a trustee for the charity the Judy Murray Foundation, which helps children access and excel in tennis.)

I still sometimes look back at my own life and wonder, if I'd made different choices when I was playing, if I'd been braver, how good could I have been? The tennis world was very different 40 years ago. There was no academy or even full-time trainers in Scotland. So for me then, tennis was just a hobby I got quite good at. Only 1 per cent of women played tennis in Scotland then. It was not a viable career. I had to travel to find competitions. I had to travel abroad myself a lot at 17 and that was tough. I had to organise it all myself, coach myself, travel a lot. Probably I wasn't good enough to make a career of it anyway but there were no opportunities in Scotland to help me find out. And I wasn't tough or mature enough to do what I had to abroad.

I had my purse stolen from my bag in Barcelona one day when I was away for a tennis tournament – all my money, my tickets, my passport, my hotel key – and I suddenly realised how alone I was. This was before ATMs or mobile phones. I had to go to the British Embassy for help. And when I got home my dad said, no, that's enough. I hate to quit on anything but the truth is, I think I was glad he said that. It must have been so worrying for them every time I went away. When I was at school I was also offered a tennis scholarship in Virginia and I didn't go. I think back now and think, oh, I wish I'd have been brave enough to do that. It would have given me the chance to grow up, to learn so much about the sport and that kind of life.

Due to inexperience, wanting my son to have opportunities I hadn't taken, and being flattered by the attention of people telling me how special he was, I made a mistake sending my son away from home too soon. Jamie was young and innocent, dreaming of being a tennis player. I knew he wouldn't get the opportunities in Scotland he was being offered in Cambridge. I'd do things very differently if I'd known then what I know now; taking a child out of a comfortable, safe, caring environment, away from friends, family, known coaches, it didn't work out the way the LTA promised it would. Six months later, we brought him home. It damaged his confidence and his game. He didn't play at all for a few months when he came home, though he came back eventually. But it caused a lot of anguish. Fortunately, he came out of the other side and now he's got his Grand Slam titles and had his number 1 doubles ranking. But I learned from that mistake and waited till Andy was 15 before I let him train abroad (he went on to win three Grand Slams and was awarded an OBE in 2013).

I haven't been able to watch Andy or Jamie on TV for years. I find it too stressful. I can't help, I can't do anything. I just ask someone to text me when it's all over. I don't go to the matches as often as I used to either, it's just too stressful, all the expectation and the pressure on them. I find that very difficult. I'd love to be able to enjoy it more. But when I'm there, no matter how hard it is, I can't get up and leave. Even if I feel like I'm having a heart attack I can't slide under the seat or walk out. Because, just like they did when they were little, they still look up for reassurance and support and encouragement. That's why you're there, not to make them feel worse by looking scared or worried.

It's hard hearing people in the media attack Andy's personality. You just have to keep reminding yourself the people who write articles criticising Andy's personality or the way he looks or his behaviour generally haven't ever met him. They don't know anything about him. I reassure myself with that. I only care about the opinion of people who know us, who care about us, who love us. The rest is just words.

I've read an enormous amount of rubbish about me. And it is upsetting. At first I read everything because I wanted to know who was saying what. The sporting world is full of male journalists, male photographers, and male editors. Right from the start they've chosen to use pictures of me baring my teeth or pumping my fists, looking scary or aggressive. So people only ever saw me in the most stressful situations, and I am very sensitive and I do show my emotions. The media built an image of me as this angry tiger mother. I used to get angry letters at the house, written in very spidery writing to suggest a very elderly hand. And they said it was terrible, aggressive 'awful behaviour'.

I think people are uncomfortable with the unusual dynamic of a mother and sons. It's not common in sport. I never asked for any attention. I was just a mother watching her sons play tennis. The same as I'd been since they were seven years old.

I think doing *Strictly Come Dancing* was really good for me. It showed people there was more to me than a competitive tennis coach, or just Jamie and Andy's mum. In the last four or five years I've come away from working at the very top end of the sport, and I'm doing much more grass roots work, and hopefully that's also helped people see another side of me. One that has a life outside Wimbledon!

Dunblane has always been enormously supportive and enormously proud of everything Jamie and Andy have done. The boys don't get back very often but they still think of Dunblane as home. I think their success brought a lot of excitement and joy to the town and I think that's helped a bit with the recovery (since the primary school massacre in 1996). It's good to think that people round the word now think of Dunblane with happy associations, and not just as a place of tragedy.

I think my 16-year-old self would be amazed by what her sons have achieved. The Davis Cup victories, winning Wimbledon – that would have been such a huge thing to that teenage Scottish tennis lover. Back then you were lucky if tennis got one line in the sports round-up in the *Glasgow Herald* or *The Scotsman*. It was absolutely a minority sport. Now, against a backdrop of no support for tennis anywhere in the country, this little Scottish town has produced two world champions. And sometimes we even get onto the front page.

On a more personal note, the teenage me would be happy to see how her confidence and courage grew so much she was able to do a show like *Strictly Come Dancing*. Looking glamorous and completely sequinned-up on national Saturday night TV! I didn't have a lot of confidence as a teenager. I had no interest in what I looked like. I would never stand up in class or ask a question. I was very quiet, didn't like to be looked at or singled out. I didn't feel attractive. And even after that, I didn't have time or the money to go and buy fashionable clothes. But in later life, just these last few years, I've had more money and more time and I've come to enjoy going to the spa, learning how to put on make-up, shopping for nice clothes. And that would come as a huge surprise to the younger me in her hoodie and trainers.

Keeley Hawes

Actor

10 April 2017

I started going to Sylvia Young's theatre school at the age of nine so I knew I enjoyed acting. But I wasn't part of the acting world. The school happened to move into premises across from my house at a time when I was really enjoying being in the primary school play. If they hadn't, I probably wouldn't have gone to that school. I wouldn't have known such a thing existed. There were no actors in my family – my dad's a black cab driver. There were six of us in the house in the estate in Marylebone being brought up by one person and we didn't have a lot of money. I got a grant to go to the school. It was quite an unusual situation, I suppose.

I left school at age 16 without much of an idea what to do next. There are about 250 pupils every year at Sylvia Young. I could name about five or six who've gone on to have great careers since we left. Not everyone walks into fantastic jobs. And I always felt there were other people better than me in the room. I was quite an awkward teenager, partly because I got very tall very quickly, taller than a lot of the boys. So I felt very out of place for a while. I went back to the school about a year after leaving and a boy who'd been in my year did a double-take before he recognised me. He said, 'God, you didn't look like that at school!' Not that I looked fabulous, I'd just lost that gawky gangly teenager look.

I felt a bit adrift when I left school. I applied for college and soon realised it wasn't for me. But I wasn't sure what was. When I look at my 16-year-old son now I think, how is anyone supposed to know what they want to do for the rest of their life at the age of 16? You feel grown-up but I know now what a baby you still are at that age. I had a few part-time jobs. I wanted a car so I worked in McDonald's in the evening, a supermarket at the weekends. I wanted my own money and I felt a great sense of achievement when I got my weekly pay cheques. And I learned to drive at 17; I remember clearly that feeling of independence when I got into a car and thought, now I can go anywhere.

If I bumped into my 16-year-old self now I'd think, what the hell is going on with the purple dungarees from Camden Market? It was only when I modelled for six months that I began to get a clue how to dress. I got a bit better, but not a lot. I wasn't drinking or smoking. I was quite boring, I think – my parents wouldn't have had much to worry about. I didn't have a boyfriend until I was 17. No one was very interested. I think it was a bit of an ugly duckling thing. I mean, looking back I wasn't ugly, but it took a while for things to fall into place. And then I was scouted in the street by a model agency. It took me by complete surprise, I had no idea such things existed. But actually, I had a lovely six months making friends and travelling, though I wasn't the greatest model.

My first adult acting job came completely out of the blue. I had an idea in my head that I might go to drama school when I was 18. But before that could happen, I was working in the fashion department at *Cosmo* magazine and I distinctly remember I was going through a shoe cupboard when I got a phone call to say someone had seen my picture in (the trade magazine) *Spotlight*. They invited me to audition for what turned out to be Dennis Potter's last work, *Karaoke*. And I got it. There was a lot of publicity surrounding it and from there I got an agent and my career began. Suddenly I was an adult with a proper job.

I'd love to go back and tell my 16-year-old self she'll be nominated for a BAFTA one day. That would save her a lot of worry. She'd be amazed that I've managed to continue to work as an actor all this time. She's not got too long to wait until she does *Spooks* (the long-running spy drama) – I was in my early twenties then. Being in that kind of hit show would really excite her. You can never foresee what's going to happen with shows like *Line of Duty* or *The Missing*, there's no recipe for that kind of success. It's really fantastic to be involved in something with that level of writing. I just read the scripts and knew I wanted to be involved. Yes, I've been very lucky.

I never considered anything but having children. It never occurred to me that I wouldn't. My children were all planned. I had my son when I was 24. That doesn't seem that young to me. I'd had all my three children by the time I was thirty. I loved motherhood immediately, it's the best thing that's ever happened to me. I like to think I have quite a cool, relaxed relationship with my children, but though we're not generations apart, I'm still their mum and probably not as cool as I'd like to think. We all sit together every Friday night to watch the US sitcom *Modern Family*. And my big boy and I watched the TV drama *Breaking Bad* together. It does make things hard regarding work because you do disappear for a year and a half with every child. And that's a long time in this business. But there was never any question that's what I wanted to do.

If I could go and relive any time in my life, it would be back to having one of my children. Any one of them would do. I'd just love to make the most of such a special time, with my husband (actor Matthew Macfadyen) by my side, as was my first husband (Spencer McCallum) when I had our son. It's over so quickly, and you have lots of worries about whether you're doing it right to come in the future. But for that little moment, it's just perfect.

Jess Phillips

Member of Parliament

5 February 2018

At 16, I was a raver, a party animal to say the least. Weekends would start early on a Friday night, round at my friend's house where we'd get ready. Then we'd be out, maybe to a local party at someone's house. Then on Saturday it was an all-night rave until the wee small hours of Sunday. School was okay. I didn't get into fights but I stood up to people in power, often. So I did get into trouble. If I was being scolded for something I hadn't done, I wouldn't let up defending myself. Once a teacher threw a chair at me.

I started going out with a boy right after my 16th birthday. I went out with him for five years. It was horrendous at many points throughout. We split up and got back together lots of times. It took me a long time not to feel I'd wasted the formative years of my life with him. I went on holiday with my friend Marcella after we broke up and she made me say a nice thing about him every day so I didn't feel I'd wasted five years of my life. Five years, all through university, as I was becoming an adult – I couldn't stop thinking about all the other things I could have done.

I turned 16 in 1997, when Tony Blair's Labour government got in. My parents were very left-wing and I'd been heavily involved in the campaign. My house was one of the places it was run from. Even my frail old grandad was out canvassing and handing out leaflets. So we had a real street party vibe for the weeks running up to the election. I remember vividly us all sitting down to watch the results coming in – me and my three brothers and our friends upstairs – the adults getting gradually drunk downstairs. When Portillo lost his seat you could hear my dad cheering all through the house. The next night my parents had a house party which went on all weekend. We revelled in it for hours and hours. I was born under Thatcher, I'd only known a Tory government. It felt genuinely life-changing.

If I was to tell my 16-year-old self about how the Labour Party has developed since, how would she feel? I think she would be depressed about some of the things which have happened but also really proud. The things I cared about were women's rights and equality and I think the Labour government did loads to push women forward. Things got better for women under Labour. But in 2005 my parents left the Labour Party due to the war in Iraq. They'd been paying my annual fees so when they left, I ended up leaving too. And I didn't seek to rejoin for a long time.

My mum died in 2011. I actually rejoined the party in 2010 during the leadership election, when Ed Miliband was elected. My mum regretted voting for Tony Blair as leader, rather than someone more left-wing. She knew she was dying so she didn't think it was worth re-joining so I re-joined and voted for Ed Miliband on her behalf. My dad re-joined too. He's painfully proud of me when he's talking to other people – he must be a real pain in the neck actually – but to me he'll just say, you did well. We come from a very working-class background where there's this almost superstitious feeling that if you put someone on a pedestal you'll lose them.

When Jo (her friend Jo Cox MP) was murdered, my family really struggled. Especially my three brothers. When I get abuse on social media or anywhere they can get very 'I'm coming down to have a fucking word if you ever talk to my sister like that again'. One of my brothers was particularly upset. He rang me up and said, 'I thought it was you, I really thought it was you.'

My teenage self wouldn't be surprised that I became an MP, I think that maybe I always thought I would do that. But she would be shocked that I had children so young. I used to be sure I'd be an amazing human rights lawyer or something incredible, a real career woman. The fact that I had babies when I was 22, that would shock the girl who went on marches for the rights of women to have abortions. I had this moment just after my son was born of, oh my God, I've got a baby, what was I thinking? My now husband and I had only been together a few weeks, though I'd known him all of my adult life. I found early motherhood horrendous. I mean, I loved Harry, though if I'm honest that took a while – I love him much more now – but I found it really, really hard. It was lonely and crushing at times. I felt a lot of guilt, I wasn't good enough. But in the long term, I think I handled it well. We carved out a good life together.

I didn't get into politics seriously until 2011. I was working with Women's Aid and I got involved with government policy. And I really liked it. Around the same time, my mum died. Maybe I thought, right, I've got to get on with life. And it was a distraction; it's sad when your mum dies. And she was a campaigner. Her friends get in touch quite a lot and tell me how proud she would be of what I'm doing now. But I know that. She would be immensely proud. I have so much of her, she's like a coat I keep on. I've always thought, I would give all of my life's earnings, my house, everything, just to have one more phone call with her. But no more so than since I became an MP.

I think it's an achievement that I became someone that people listen to. I don't think my children are my greatest achievement – they're their own achievement. Sometimes I think they're good in spite of the fact that I'm their mum. I think maybe my relationship with my husband might be my greatest achievement. We have total equality. I see very few examples of real partnerships in relationships and we definitely have that.

If I could go back to any time in my life and live it again, I'd go to a moment in 2010 when I was in the car with my husband and my sons. We were on the way to see my mum. My second son was about one year old. When he was born, I felt like he completed the square. I remember thinking in the car, we all fit in this one tiny space together. This is my life, these people I love and want to spend my time with. And this is all we need.

Susie Dent

Lexicographer and etymologist

6 November 2020

My main interest when I was 16... well, certainly not boys. I went to a convent, which was all-girls, and I didn't have any brothers so I felt slightly intimidated by boys. They were a complete mystery to me. I found them kind of noisy and not people I wanted to mix with. Which is very strange, I loved music and I was quite interested in clothes. But I was definitely nerdy as well, before it became fashionable to be a geek.

I was really into my work. My parents divorced when I was 13 and I'd always lived mostly in my head but that was the moment when I decided I needed a safe space for all my worries. And it was very obvious where that space was going to be – in work and in words. I think I escaped the real sadness of it that way. It was a huge coping mechanism for me. I still find that being a word detective and trying to unravel the words people choose, it takes me away from everything.

When I was about 13, I felt really sad and wrote a secret diary about feeling awful and not seeing the point of life. I definitely didn't feel suicidal but I was very, very melancholy. But by the time I was 16 I think I was a lot more upbeat, quite happy in myself. I've always enjoyed my own company, and I think I'd got through it all by then. If you find something you are passionate about I'm not sure it really matters if you don't have lots of friends. I was always an eavesdropper and an observer and I think to be a linguist, you have to have an ear out, always listening to things that people are saying or writing. I remember my mum saying, 'Oh my giddy aunt' and thinking, 'Who, what aunt, what does she mean?' And I'd jot it down in my notebook to investigate.

The biggest things in my life have come to me by chance. I joined Oxford University Press when I came back from studying in America (she obtained a master's degree in German at Princeton University, New Jersey) and I didn't know they had an arrangement with *Countdown* (the long-running TV gameshow on which she is a contributor) and ITV. That wasn't on my radar at all. When I was asked to do it, I said no quite a few times and then, thank God, my boss insisted that I go and audition. I'm so grateful to him for that. I think the younger me would be really grateful to know that somehow fate has swung in my favour on a few occasions. And that I've been able to indulge this passion all my life.

I've always been quite happy below the radar so I definitely didn't jump at the chance of going on TV. Also, I just assumed that I would be absolutely rubbish at it. And in fact the evidence for me being right about that is there on YouTube, where you can see my fairly rubbish first performance. I was frozen with fear, and that made me look slightly arrogant. I really wasn't, I was just so nervous. I barely moved my head.

I think the big blight on my life has been worry. About health, money, my kids, those kind of things. As Rachel Riley will tell you, because she's brilliant at telling me to stop. But I do let worries spiral. As ever with me, it's all internalised so I don't really talk about it very much. But I really wish I didn't have that. I feel like I've wasted so much effort and energy and brainpower on worrying that something bad is going to happen. Sometimes living in your head isn't always a good thing if your head is absolutely full of anxiety.

Strangely, I didn't take any time at all to get used to being a mother. It felt so instinctive and spontaneous, the whoosh people talk about. Motherhood is definitely the best thing I've ever experienced and, probably the best thing I've ever done in my life. I'm so lucky because I know not everyone has that. It's a real privilege to feel that immediate bond. If anything, I probably feel it too strongly because it makes me want to protect my girls from absolutely everything. I realise that I've got to start letting go. It's been a bit easier since my eldest went to university. She's completely independent now, and I don't know what she's up to day to day, even though we talk a lot. So I've kind of navigated that one and I think I've got to the other side, which is good. But it's a really tough thing to have to do.

If I could tell my younger self one thing it would be, don't worry about what people think. I'm hugely self-conscious and always have been. I hate being photographed with a passion. Google Images is awash with horrendous pictures of me or of me running away from the camera. It's something I always say to everybody else and never take my own advice on, that it doesn't matter if other people criticise you. I was quite nervous about going on Twitter for example because I immediately thought I was going to be trolled. I remember really steeling myself to look at notifications. But actually I tend to get followed by people who are equally passionate about words and that's brilliant because it's enabled me to have this real connection with some lovely people I never would have met. But I had this fear that people were going to think badly of me.

There's so many downsides to social media but one of the really good things about it is that it enables people to be themselves and to celebrate being different, not being run of the mill, and not fitting into a norm. I think it's brilliant for people who want to find other less conventional people who are like them.

When it comes to things like comedy – *8 out of 10 Cats Does Countdown* – I'd tell myself you don't have to try to be someone you're not. In the beginning I was really worried that I wasn't funny so what was I doing on the show? In the actual recording the audience get 40 minutes of really, really funny quips from the comedians and they'll be laughing their heads off, before Jimmy (Carr) even introduces me. And I used to think, oh God, I can't let the humour drop, I've got to be funny. And it took me a while to realise that actually, that's not what I'm there for. I'm not funny and that's fine. I'm normally only funny by mistake.

If I could go back and relive any moment in my life, a moment of real, real happiness... I was in New York taking the Staten Island Ferry, and I was on my own. I saw the Statue of Liberty, it was incredibly sunny, the sea was sparkling and I had everything I needed. I felt totally free of any worry as to what might happen; everything was perfect in that moment.

I haven't thought about that moment for years but that's what suddenly sprang to mind. The swish of the water, the sun on my skin, the chatter of people around me – I just thought, yeah, this is where I want to be.

Chapter 9:

Self-image

Dawn French

Comedian and writer
9 October 2017

At 16, I was virginal. I thought about sex almost every hour of every day. Imagining it, anticipating it, fearing it and longing for it. I was at a girls' school and my brother was at a boys' school so I fell in love with each of his friends in turn. Mostly misguided crushes on inappropriate people. Always asking, when will the moment happen? Before that I'd practised kissing on plums, other girls, pillows. I feel very affectionate about the teenage me. I was full of hope, always looking for the good in every moment. And always looking for the laugh.

There were points when I didn't have much confidence. It would go from high to low a lot. My dad gave me a bit of a talking to one night, when I was off to a party in my purple suede hot pants. He told me what I was to him. A beauty and a prize. He said if anything happened to me he'd be devastated. He told me any boy would be lucky to have me. And I utterly believed him. He was probably handling me carefully, knowing I was a bit vulnerable, off to a party, maybe not with a lot of confidence. But I believed he spoke the truth and it really stuck with me. A dad's boost of confidence to his daughter is a very potent thing. I was very lucky to have him. And I still believe what he said to me was, and is, true.

I was eighteen when my dad committed suicide. If I could go back and put an arm round my teenage self I'd say, one day, eventually, you will understand this. Because it was so hard to understand then. It was a giant trauma. I was angry, confused, bewildered, sad, blaming all the wrong people, including myself. But as time has gone on I've learned about mental health, and understood that if my dad had perhaps lived in a time when he didn't feel so ashamed of his depression, it might have been very different. It's a cliche but it's true – over time you learn to forgive that person and understand they sought a way out at a particular time. At that point, for him, life was a sort of hell. He was just then altered, and not the dad I knew.

It wasn't until the middle part of my life that I began worrying and catastrophising. Probably to do with having kids. Paying mortgages. Having responsibilities. I longed for children and I was so happy when it happened, but when they were there the responsibility sometimes felt overpowering. It can wear you down if you're not careful. Since then, I've made conscious decisions to live differently. There's a Jane Hirshfield poem where she says, 'I move my chair into the sun'. That has been the most useful thing I've learned in the last ten years. You actually can choose to move out to where it's warmer. And now, it's like muscle memory, I'm starting to feel much more optimistic again. I'm back to where I was when I was young.

The 16-year-old me would be amazed and very impressed that I ended up in the comedy world with comedians I adored. I still have odd starstruck moments, like when I met Michael Palin or John Cleese, and I thought, oh God, I have adored you. And I have to tell myself, come on, they're just people, they're normal. Among people I actually knew, Rik Mayall was very easy to love. Not only was he beautiful, he was extremely funny in a very unique way. He used to have me in absolute fits of laughter. Probably because he performed very easily in his normal everyday life. He would do anything, any stupid thing, to get a laugh out of you. He was a complete tart for a laugh. I have a lot to thank him for.

It can be hard when a friend, especially one you've never done any work separately from, suddenly has a huge success without you. *Ab Fab* was such a massive hit. Until then Jennifer (Saunders, her comedy partner since the early eighties) and I had been utterly linked in everything we did. I was made very aware that, in comedy terms, she was a completely individual, separate person. With her own powers. That really shocked me. Not only was she able to do it without me, she could do it really well. So that was really annoying. But however jealous I was, I love her and I was proud of her. I dealt with it by being open and honest about my jealousy. I sent her a bunch of flowers when she won a BAFTA saying, 'Congratulations you cunt.'

For me, our separation was a sad thing (she split with husband Lenny Henry in 2010, after 26 years together), and a kind of waking up to the inevitable. That's a slow and painful process, when you finally start listening to your inner instinct. You must never, never ignore voices that are in your heart. We all know them. We suppress them like mad, but sometimes they are the truth. So it was sad. But we handled it by acknowledging that we were both in a bit of pain. And we looked after each other. We were kind to each other. Those were the brilliant things and I was delighted with that. It's not like we had to say, ooh, let's try to be kind to each other. We just were, because we'd always been. We thought, let's finish this as we started it, as friends. And we've got a kid! Who matters much more than us. And she must never feel that she was trapped in the middle of this, or that she was for one minute to blame.

If I could have one last conversation with anyone, it would be my dad. Though I've always felt he knows what's been happening in my life because I have him in my back pocket at all times, sort of like my engine. But I would like to talk to him about his struggles with mental health. I knew nothing about them at the time, though other people did. But it was such a shameful thing back then, no one talked about it. Most of the time he was a cheerful, funny, adventurous, happy dad. Then there were times when he withdrew to a dark room, but I just thought he had a migraine. I'd like to talk to him properly now about he was feeling. Now that I think I understand.

If I could go back to any moment in my life, I'd be 18 again, in a tent, in the dunes on a Cornwall beach called Gwithian Sands. That was the moment everything I had been worrying about for years finally came to pass in that intimate little tent with a lovely, lovely boy I met. It was not at all traumatising. It was a happy event. Then we had a big, long sloppy kiss. And then we went for a big swim in the sea. And then we had a Fab ice lolly. Bliss.

Clare Balding

Broadcaster and journalist

4 March 2013

I was quite a stroppy teenager, quite difficult. Horses and dogs kept me grounded and connected. I think I was gentler and kinder to animals than people at that age. I'd gone through a difficult period at school when I was in quite a lot of trouble. I got caught shoplifting and got suspended at school. I was very upset and discombobulated by that experience. Thinking back to it still upsets me. It took me a long time to get over it. I think I was trying to fit in with the cool gang, trying to be like everyone else. It's a tribal instinct, isn't it, you feel safer if you don't stand out, if you're part of the group.

I think life is about learning to be an individual and finding out who you really are. If I could talk to my young self now I'd say, be confident, you'll be good enough, you don't have to fit in. And be brave enough to be different, in whatever way you are. I was very interested in boys at school. Again, I thought I had to be like everyone else. So I had boyfriends. In that regard, I was a late bloomer.

I wouldn't say I had an eating disorder. But for the purposes of trying to hit a target weight as a jockey, I completely disrespected my body. I did whatever I needed to do to lose 3 pounds in a day. As well as not eating or drinking much, I did a lot of running in a sweatsuit – I worked hard but I also took a lot of shortcuts, including laxatives and making myself sick. But you know, you get through these things. Now I eat healthily and exercise and look after myself.

If I met my young self now, I'd think she was a bit insecure and unsure of what her life was about and who she was. But some things remain the same – she's not afraid of hard work and generally quite positive about things and has high energy levels, and that's still true of me. The young me would be surprised at the variety of my work now. She expects to be a lawyer or work in marketing. And she'd be surprised by my having any sort of public profile. That would frighten her. But then, it frightens me now, it's terrifying. I certainly never wanted to be famous. In many ways I still don't.

If I was to give my young self advice on dealing with the media, I'd say, remember, none of this is real. What's real is love, how you live, the influence you can have. A critic's view of your performance is not real, it's not lasting. It's real in their heads – probably – but don't overreact to criticism or praise because somewhere in the middle is the truth. You get re-booked if you're good. And make yourself easy to work with. I'm a big believer in respecting other people's time. I'd tell my 16-year-old self, your time is no more precious than anyone else's. So don't be late, don't waste people's time, never think you're better than anyone else.

When I got my cancer diagnosis, I buried my head in the sand a bit and pretended it wasn't happening, because that's the way I deal with things. I didn't want any sympathy so I didn't tell anyone. I couldn't deal with that look in people's eyes; 'poor you'. Actually, I realise now, people need to share it with you and I wasn't very generous about letting people do that. But Alice (her partner) and my mum were absolutely brilliant. Alice did a lot of investigation on the medical side, finding out about treatments, while I was just carrying on as if it wasn't happening.

If I could turn the clock back to any time I'd relive the whole of the London 2012 Olympics. If I could do it all again, and make it go slower, I would. I absolutely loved every minute. But it already seems so long ago.

Cherie Booth

Barrister and writer
30 April 2020

At 16, I had long hair in pigtails and was terribly thin and gawky. I certainly wasn't a sporty kid but I was good at public speaking and drama and singing so that was the way I could be popular. I went to what they call a direct grant grammar school – there were 70 children in my primary school year and two girls got into this grammar school. Most of the children in my grammar school were better off than I was. They weren't rich – this was a Catholic grammar school in a suburb of Liverpool – they were just better off than us. And they certainly didn't come from a single-parent family as I did. So I was very conscious that the only way I was going to get anywhere was if I could succeed, and at that time success was defined as doing well at exams. So that was my focus.

I think I got my outgoing trait from my parents. They met when they were actors on tour. My mother had to give up her acting when my sister was born, and then when my father (well-known TV actor Tony Booth) abandoned us, when I was eight, she had to take up a job in a fish and chip shop. Thank goodness we had my grandmother, my father's mother, who helped out with the childcare and gave us a roof over our heads. But it was difficult. I don't remember my mum really having many new clothes, she spent all her money on my sister and I. My mother left school at 14 because her own mother died, and she had to look after her ten-year-old brother and her father, who was a miner. My mum loved him, he was self-taught, he was a poet. My mum loved literature and my paternal grandmother loved reading so we weren't a household that didn't have books. And my grandma always had a very strong sense of justice and right and wrong. We were always very politically aware. I joined the Labour Party when I was 16.

I didn't really consider being an actor because I'd seen the effect of my father's precarious career – he was very successful but sadly he spent it all on what he described as 'drink and crumpet'. I was very conscious of all the sacrifices my mum and grandma made and I wanted to make sure that I had a job that would bring me financial security so I could share that financial security with them. My then boyfriend's mother said to me, 'Cherie, you've always been good at debating, why don't you think about being a lawyer?' I had no idea what that meant or involved. I'd never met anyone who was a lawyer. But I thought, that sounds like a way of using my speaking skills and at the same time, earning money.

Very few people were divorced in those days so it was a big thing to deal with when my father left my mother. He was quite famous, about to get onto *Till Death Us Do Part* (the popular sitcom of the '60s and '70s). And my grandma's cousin was our local parish priest so that didn't necessarily help either. Also, without a working father we had much less money. But in another way I was very lucky because my grandfather – my dad's father – was alive. He was very fond of my mother. I don't think he really forgave my father for abandoning her. Even before my father left, I was brought up very much as part of his family. Sometimes I wasn't entirely sure whether my dad was my dad or my bigger brother.

The 16-year-old me used to say she was going to be the first woman prime minister. So maybe she would be surprised to find out that I never was. Or maybe she'd be surprised that I actually did make it to 10 Downing Street, albeit on my husband's coat tails. Though the better way to get there would be to do it yourself, of course. Maybe she'd be amazed that I did become a QC like one of her heroes, Rose Heilbron, the Liverpudlian woman who was the very first female QC.

If I could go back and give my young self advice it might be to understand, which I didn't until I went to the bar to do my pupillage, that in this world it's not just about how much you know, it's also about who you know. And I didn't know anyone. I definitely felt the imposter syndrome at times. Just little things like going to eat the dinners at Lincoln's Inn (the London-based, very prestigious body of lawyers) – they presented port at the end and I had no idea what it was. I just didn't know the etiquette of lots of things. I only realise now that a lot of what we were doing in the Halls and Lincoln's Inn was what they did in Oxford colleges and public schools but they were completely alien environments to me.

He managed to charm me eventually, but when I first met Tony (Tony Blair, who later went on to serve as prime minister of the UK from 1997 to 2007) we were rivals for the same scholarship. And then for the same place in chambers. My pupil master said to me, 'Cherie, there's only one place here and there's a boy and there's a girl and, obviously, we have to go for the boy.' I knew more about the law than he did, but of course it was a disadvantage being a woman, especially a working-class woman with a Liverpool accent. In those days people just said he was a better bet. Which just goes to show how wrong stereotypes can be because I'm still a practising lawyer 45 years on and he gave up the law after seven years for some other career entirely.

I hadn't realised when Tony became prime minister that there would be such interest in me. And then of course Tony and I were quite different from our predecessors. I was the first prime minister's spouse to have gone to university. It just wasn't the thing for women to do that. We were also different in that we had a young family, our kids went to the local state school. So there was a lot of interest in all of that. I became conscious about what I wore, how I looked. I did quite a lot of high-profile cases as a lawyer, but there you're judged by your successes or otherwise in court – with the wig and gown, it's not a beauty contest. So it was a bit different being in the public eye when no one was interested in what you said. In fact, you weren't supposed to say anything. People tended to focus on how you look. So if I could give my younger self advice, I'd say learn how to do your hair and make-up.

If I could have one last conversation with anyone, it's a hard choice between my mother or my grandmother. My mother, who I owe so much to, saw me become a QC, and she saw us going to Downing Street. She came with me when we met the Pope, she met the Queen. We did all sorts of things that neither of us would ever have dreamed of. But my own grandmother died in 1987, so she only saw me become a barrister, she didn't see those other things. I always remember the first time I went with Tony to the Vatican, to see Pope John Paul, and we got the official visit, and I could hear my grandma in my head as I was walking down the corridors of the Vatican, saying, well, we might not have had a priest in the family but our Cherie met the Pope.

If I could go back to any time and live it again it would have to be, for us as a family, the moment in '97 when we won the election. There was a series of events, starting with the exit poll, then going over to Tony's seat. And seeing that my old seat (she stood for Labour in North Thanet in 1983, losing to Tory candidate Roger Gale), which had been Tory the whole time I was growing up, had become a Labour seat that night. That was an amazing moment. We came back to London and the dawn broke, and the sun came up and we went into the gathering of the Labour Party members and realised that after so many years of Tory rule, we actually had a chance to make things better.

Caitlin Moran

Writer
16 July 2020

At 16, I knew I wanted to be a writer. In fact, I was already a writer, I'd published my first book, a children's novel and I was just starting to work for *Melody Maker*. That was quite weird, turning up at a cool rock magazine having written a children's book. I was trying to project the aura of being a sassy rock 'n' roll lady, so at the first editorial meeting I turned up with a pack of cigarettes and a bottle of Southern Comfort, and I threw them down on the table and said, 'Who wants a shot?' because I thought that's what grown-ups did. And all the grown-ups around the table were like, who is this mad child monkey in a dress? We're trying to have an editorial meeting.

I had big plans when I was 16. I was in a three-bedroom council house in Wolverhampton with seven other siblings, and at that point we had 18 dogs because my parents were breeding dogs. I was sharing the double bed that my nan had died in with my three-year-old sister, who persistently wet the bed. So when movies were telling me that teenage girls were going off to the prom and having their sweet sixteens, I was lying in bed, wearing my dad's thermal underwear that was wet from my sister's urine, thinking, I'm gonna make a better life for myself.

I got interviewed when I was 16, and the journalist, Valerie Grove, said I came across as very arrogant, that I would talk myself up a lot and dismiss other people who weren't our family. Because obviously I felt massively insecure; we were dirt poor, I only had three items of clothing. I was aware that I smelled quite a lot. So I had to play up this whole thing of like, yeah, this is how we are and it's cool and it doesn't matter if I'm poor and fat and ugly because I'm really fucking clever and I'm gonna tell you ten jokes now. If you're a wise person, you would have seen that I was very insecure and scared and smelly. And if you were just taking me on surface, you'd probably think I was an annoying prick.

I was still a virgin at 16 so I was very interested in getting kissed and having sex and touching boys. The problem with being home educated, as we were, is that you can't really have any kind of early teenage crushes because you only have access to your brothers and that would be wrong. So the first time I had access to men was when I became a journalist and started to interview them. To me at 16 this seemed like a magic thing – you could ring up a person called a press officer and go, I'd like to meet Evan Dando from the Lemonheads at 11 o'clock on Thursday, and then Evan Dando would be delivered to my pub table. And I would think, well, I should probably get off with him because this is an opportunity. Unfortunately, most of the pop stars that were delivered to pubs for me to interview were profoundly not interested in that happening. So I went through a process of trying to get off with rock stars, and they were very firmly 'no'. You would think as a child going out to meet rock stars they'd just be pigs, kind of like bumming you in a hotel. But actually they were all so respectful and treated me like a little sister and looked after me.

I don't think my 16-year-old self would be very surprised by anything that's happened to me. I absolutely have lived the life I presumed I would when I was 16. When I read the novels of Jilly Cooper, and she described to me what a middle-class life was like, I was like, I want that. I want to live in a lovely house with a beautiful garden with herbaceous borders, surrounded by delightful spaniels, and have friends over and we'll get drunk in the garden drinking champagne, smoking fags and gossiping. I've always had really gigantic dreams so I absolutely imagined a future of film premieres and books being published.

I had massive social anxiety due to being raised at home and never talking to anybody. I wish I could go back to the earliest point where I started socialising and tell myself I didn't need to drink and smoke in order to talk to other people. That has taken so long to try and reverse – I don't think I spoke to anybody not drunk and not smoking a cigarette until probably two years ago. I'm a lightweight so I've been to amazing celebrity parties going around talking to all my heroes and I've just been the twat that fell over backwards into a hedge. And then sent an email to Jimmy Carr or Jonathan Ross the next day going, I'm so sorry. I haven't been invited back since so I just want to tell them I'm not a problematic drinker anymore, I've cured my social anxiety.

I'd tell my younger self what every girl needs to hear; don't go out with a troubled boy and think you can save him. Don't think that you are the mender of a broken person and the more you love someone, the better they will get. They won't. I think the thing women find hardest to believe is that someone who's supposed to love them doesn't love them. Whether it's your parents or an abusive partner. I think if someone says they're your boyfriend, you presume that they must love you. So everything that is happening to you is love. And it's not. Those people don't love you, they're just abusing you. And the harder you try, the smaller and more broken and the more upset you're going to get.

When it comes to love, art is a very bad advisor. In the early '90s I was listening to the Afghan Whigs and Nick Cave, who were writing about sex and love being dark and dangerous. They're not songs about true love, they're songs about unrequited love or dysfunctional love. And so when I met Pete (Paphides, her husband, who she's been with since she was 19), because he wasn't a dangerous fucked-up dark boy I just presumed he was a mate. I knew I felt more comfortable around him than anyone else; I didn't have to pretend to be anyone, I didn't have to drink or smoke. It took my subconscious about two years to just go, oh for fucksake, and make me have a dream where we were going on an escalator together, and the escalator just went on and on and on and on forever. And I turned to him and said, 'What's happening here?', and he said, 'It's okay, we're just going to stay together till the top.' And I woke up and went, I'm in love with him, we're gonna stay together forever. So thanks unconscious for stepping in there, because my conscious mind was too stupid to realise I was in love with him.

I think the thing about me now that would surprise the

teenage me most would be raising daughters, as cool and non-fucked up, as I have. My family was pretty dysfunctional and quite screwy, and so I just presumed that everybody had to grow up with a certain amount of screwed-up ness. But I seem to have – touch wood – raised girls who are just very happy, very confident, they can ask for what they want, they're not scared of anything. They know who they are, they can talk about anything they want to. That would be a genuine surprise to me.

If I could go back to one time in my life it would be two times. One would be Glastonbury 2010, which I spent with the best bunch of mates, blissfully happy the entire time. The other time would be, I'd go back and have my second birth again. I would happily give birth again 1,000 times. If anybody I love ever wants a surrogate, I would happily get pregnant and give birth for them. There's something quite amazing about pulling that off, and you feel pretty high afterwards. And then you look at this little thing and you think wow, who are you? Before you have kids you think you'll have a little version of you or your husband and each time you have a baby you're like, oh my God, you're you. I don't know you. What are you going to do?

Gail Porter

TV presenter
21 March 2014

I was quite a good, studious teenager until I got to 16. I got on well with most people and loved going to school. They were nice people. I miss it. When I got to 16, I noticed boys and went a bit woo-hoo! I had my first kiss at 16 and I went out with my friend's older brother, which I thought was very rebellious. When I was 17, I was going clubbing and raving. I remember going to my friend's house and we all tried Martini because we'd seen her parents drink huge glasses of it. We ended up throwing up everywhere.

I was never ever glamorous as a teenager. I was kind of tomboyish, though I do remember a puffball skirt. At 16, I was pretty chubby so I was wearing baggy shirts and jeans mostly and looked like a small ball. I didn't bother too much what people thought of me, I was having good fun, but there were times when I felt self-conscious about my weight. I had bigger boobs than everyone else, I was shorter than everybody else, I felt all out of proportion. If I met the 16-year-old Gail now, I'm sure I would like her. She's friendly, open, good-natured, likes making friends.

I didn't think about the future. Dad was thinking about me being a lawyer but I just wanted to have fun. I auditioned for a kids' show on STV and got it. A few years later I was presenting *Top of the Pops* thinking, come on, I'm actually getting paid for this?!

I was shocked when I saw the Parliament thing. (In 1999 a 60-foot photo of a naked Porter was projected onto the Houses of Parliament.) I didn't know it was going to happen, I just saw it on the news. My first thought was, my life is over. Everyone I chatted to, I thought, you've probably already seen me naked. The Queen probably bloody saw it. John Prescott was probably in the building. People started talking to my breasts. My mum wasn't too chuffed and my dad still doesn't even acknowledge it happened. I was mortified about it then but I wouldn't change it now. It was funny, it wasn't harmful. And how many other school mums have a story like that?

What I really notice now about that Parliament photo is my hair. That lovely hair. Do you know, I've kept it. I have it in a box. My daughter found it one day and said, 'Mum, what is this? Please don't say what I think you're going to say.' And I said, 'Yup, that's your mum's hair.'

Everyone wanted me to wear a wig when I lost my hair. I just thought, I have to get used to it so everyone else does too. It was hard at times; I still get hurtful comments. I was out having dinner and this guy came up and said, 'Oh my God, what happened to you?' Like I'd turned into an ogre. Sometimes I do get a bit tearful. This guy shouted out of his white van, 'Baldie!' But then the lights turned to red and he had to stop. I went up to his window and knocked on it, asked him to repeat it. He just stared ahead, wouldn't wind down his window, wouldn't acknowledge me. Big scaredy.

If I could go back and put an arm around my teenage self I'd say, you're going to get hit with hair loss, depression, your mum dying and anorexia. Do not sit around your house drinking a bottle of wine and end up in rehab. Talk to people, share things. Get a hug if you need one. Don't be on your own. Because that's what I did. I'm Scottish – I couldn't tell people I was feeling shit. You have to be strong; I was sitting there thinking, I'm bald, I'm depressed, I've got problems with my thyroid, but I'm fine. I hid under the cupboard and got worse and worse.

I'm in a good place now. I think I'm really lucky, much luckier than millions of people out there in the world. There was a time when I was losing control and things were falling apart but I'm much better now. When I became a mum things became much clearer. First thing is Honey and that's it. I was told I could never have kids, because of my anorexia. When I first did my pregnancy test, me and Dan (Hipgrave, her ex-husband) did seven tests. We just thought, nah, it can't be. So she's a little miracle.

Chapter 10:

Rebellion

Rose McGowan

Actor and activist

8 July 2019

Up until I was ten, I grew up in a religious commune (in Italy) called Children of God. But I didn't believe anything they were telling me. It's young to be so questioning but I saw that what people were preaching was not what they were doing. And it was such an intense society I got to see that hypocrisy very clearly, whereas most people get a watered-down version of it, so it takes them longer to catch on. I saw the way the men used their power over women and it made no sense to me. It still doesn't make sense.

We escaped from the commune when I was ten and moved to the United States. It was a rough time at home, with step-parents who weren't very nice. I was very scared and traumatised. That's when I invented my own planet, Planet 9, so I could escape this world and my reaction to America. I would shut my eyes and imagine my planet, and I would have melodies in my head which would soothe me. Looking back at it now, I see it was a meditation, a way to astral project out of my situation. If you could just shut your eyes and go to a better place with a beautiful energy, why wouldn't you go there?

When I was 15 I divorced my parents so I could have control of my life. I was homeless, I was on my own, and I was very lonely. I was entirely focused on just surviving. So when I started having relationships with men I wasn't set up to understand that kind of world. A lot of older men were attracted to me, which at the time I thought was cool but now I think it's creepy. I developed an eating disorder as a way of responding to the world being scary. So I could feel I was in control. Because the rest of the world seemed so wild and freaky. (McGowan got into a relationship with a man who put constant pressure on her to lose weight.) I'd like to go back to that young girl and put my arm around her. And punch that man on the nose.

If you met the 16-year-old me you'd think I was very adult for someone so young. But I was very witty and funny and warm. I knew I was very cute. And I was very precocious. I was very scared as well, but you can hide fear behind a lot of things. And I've always had this inner core of strength. I've always resented being afraid and my response is to lean into the fear. I became used to doing that on my own. I knew I could go under any moment and I refused to.

I always knew I was destined for a big and strange life and I definitely wasn't wrong. When I was 19 my boyfriend (music label exec Brett Cantor) had just been killed and I was standing on a street corner crying and a woman came up to me and asked me if I wanted to be an actress. It was a really brutal time. A really good person lost his life. It's very hard to grieve someone who is murdered because it's such a strange and big thing. I went into a deep depression. But I worked out if I did this movie (*California Man*, 1992), it would get me enough money to get an apartment, so I wouldn't be homeless. And being homeless again was always the biggest terror for me. So I took my first acting job.

If I could give the younger me advice I'd say don't go into Hollywood. I didn't relate to the people around me. Their concerns were not my concerns, I had much bigger concerns. I wish I had known I was an artist earlier in my life, but Hollywood is a kind of cult which makes you think their way is the only way to do things. And since I didn't know anything about any other industry I got stuck in this dog-eat-dog world. But now I don't care what they say and I don't care what they think. I have shut the door on working in Hollywood. And they have shut the door on me. And that's okay because I'm an artist and when I was working in Hollywood I really felt that I was a commodity which wasn't worth much. But I always thought I had something of value and I think Planet 9 – the visuals, the album, and now the one-woman show – is a really significant piece of work. I think my 16-year-old self would love it. This is the outlet she was looking for; it would be beautiful to let her know she would eventually find it.

I think it's clear that things have moved forwards since my book *Brave* (released after McGowan's 2017 accusation of rape against movie exec Harvey Weinstein, which sent ripples throughout America and is seen by many as the trigger for the #MeToo movement). And it's across all industries, not just Hollywood. My goal was a lot bigger than Hollywood. I called my book *Brave* to show people how to be brave in their own lives and how to fight the machine. Because when you do fight the machine it fights back and you have to be prepared for that. I had spies infiltrate my life, I had people paid to write nasty things about me for years. All because someone in power wanted to abuse their power. And other people were profiting from that. It was a sick, toxic system that needed to be blown apart. And for me, social media was the way to do that.

If I had the chance of one last conversation with anyone I would love to talk to my father again. He died ten years ago. When I was writing my book I was so mad at him I didn't visit his grave for three years. But after the book came out I found my peace with him. The thing that eats away at me is that he never saw this new chapter of my life. He always hated Hollywood and he hated the men in Hollywood. He was an incredible painter and when I look at his paintings I see a really unique mind at work. I would love to be able to tell him about what I'm doing now and that I'm an artist and I can be free without the trappings of Hollywood. I think he would be really proud. When I travel I try to see the world through his eyes and I have a lot of conversations with him. When someone dies you can have these conversations that you were never able to have in real life.

I've become quite good at knowing when I'm in a moment I should file away and keep. So that, when times are tough and trying, I can pull out that memory and know I'm going to be okay. I was in Italy a week ago – I was born there and I feel a connection with the land. I was high on a hill by myself, looking out at the Tuscan sunset, and I felt I'd reached a moment of perfect peace. And in that moment I knew I was going to be okay.

Anna Chancellor

Actor

9 February 2013

At 16, I was just leaving school, my convent in the Dorset countryside. Looking back, it was like a whole other era, living with this old-fashioned order of Catholic nuns. We had to wear two pairs of pants. How the order of Catholic nuns had got into wearing two pairs of pants in the first place I'm not sure. The nuns had this incredible authority. I still remember hearing them in the corridor, skirts swishing, keys jangling. I'd love to play a nun now. I'd been at the convent since I was ten and I was a real underachiever intellectually, I failed every exam. I was bright and interested but I couldn't organise my brain to write ordered essays. I could talk though, I was very gregarious. I was always interested in people and had loads of friends of all ages. I had quite a lot of fun and I did lots of acting there, that was my creative relief.

When I think back I see my younger self as two things. One part was happy, up for it, liked a laugh. The other was sometimes quite depressed. I was a bit wilder than most of the other convent girls. I used to say I wanted six children to six different men. I shouldn't have done but I had a boyfriend who was much older than me, I used to sneak out to meet him and spent the weekend with him then lie on my forms, saying I'd been with my parents. Once a policeman came to speak to us in a hotel. I think my boyfriend was driving a car that had been stolen and they were following the car. He didn't arrest us but he did work out I was underage. I remember walking back to the convent that night expecting to see the police waiting for me. I don't think I've ever been so frightened in my life.

If you met the 16-year-old me now I think you'd think she was confident, but naive. You might worry about where that girl was headed. She was quite flirtatious, using all the wiles she could to get on. I think I was rather attractive. I was given this gift, this spirit, of being outgoing and being interested in other people, outward-looking. I think I'd get on with her. I have a great affinity with children, I like young people, I like young girls. I've got a daughter of course but I haven't changed from when I was a teenager – I've always liked people much younger and much older than me. Someone who knew me at 16 might not think I was much different now.

We were a modern, divorced, step-family. At times we were happy and at times it was very difficult. Seven kids thrown together – we brought each other up in some ways. I grew up in this big country house and in a way it was privileged but I found it stifling. The women didn't really work. And I longed for a close relationship with my mother. I actually really loved her but she was very cold and upper class and removed.

We lived near this bohemian artists' commune. I remember

my mum and I going to visit one of the women. She opened the cottage door and it was all cosy and warm and this little kid was wrapped up asleep in the afternoon, rather than at bedtime. And I remember wishing that was my life. I think now I must have made some deep choice then that I would fight for this kind of life, this kind of cosy mother/daughter relationship, with my own child one day. I think that's why I had a child so young, when I was just 22, without a husband.

I think my teenage self would be surprised how painful life can be. What I now realise is that the lows in life are very necessary. You don't want to go there but they are part of what makes you who you are. At 16, I wouldn't have understood how tough and how exhilarating life can be. When I was young we all took loads of drugs, that was the culture I grew up in. I understand that culture now, why you'd do that and why it's fun and why it's a kind of other form of parent. And I see what a close shave it was. It led to behaviour I don't think was truly representative of my character. But in order to stay in your true character – that takes real commitment and bravery. I have veered during my life but thank God, I think I came back to that.

I never wanted a conventional life. I found my own background incredibly stifling. I was talking to my friend earlier, who had her daughter when she was much older and was married and was in a much more conventional set-up. And I realised that that life had stability but could be very stifling for the adults – it involves routines, they have to be in bed by a certain time. It can be good for the kid but it can be depressing for the parent. I didn't have that – we would both go out late, I took her everywhere I went. We had a freedom and we really lived our experiences together. We were incredibly close, Poppy and I, but that was partly luck. Our characters fitted and we carried on along the path, staying very close. And there were times it was incredibly hard. I'd been brought up in a sort of privileged way and I found myself with a child and without those privileges. Ultimately I'm grateful for that experience, it's given me a greater depth of understanding, but at the time I was all over the place.

My first real proper acting job was probably *Four Weddings and a Funeral* (as 'Duckface'). Someone told me they were making a film about lots of fucking in the back of horseboxes and I'd be perfect for it. They clearly turned out to be wrong – about the film – but I got the job. I couldn't believe I was there. With Rowan Atkinson, Andie MacDowell and Hugh Grant – I adore him. So funny. So witty and naughty. I've always liked people like that.

I had a great time working with Peter Capaldi on *The Hour* (a TV series set in the 1950s). I felt such an affinity with Peter. We'd sit on the stairs in our old-fashioned costumes – we both looked extremely old-fashioned, from another world, and somehow I think we felt that. The scene where I told him our long-lost daughter was dead, we stood there looking at each other and we said, this is just so sad. Brilliant writing. Its writer, Abi Morgan, is genuinely interested in middle-aged women, as I am. Often you do a part and think, well this is interesting but not as interesting as my life.

The one thing I'm not crazy about myself is always being in a hurry. I long to be able to slow down and observe details. My mum lived on Exmoor and we used to go for long walks and we'd talk and swim in the river, freezing our nuts. The strange thing is, the last time I swam with her, just a few years ago, I remember driving back to London afterwards feeling unbearably sad and I didn't know why. I just had a feeling it was the last time for something. Not long after my mum got cancer and died quite quickly. And I realised that was the last time we'd ever swim together.

Eileen Atkins

Actor

23 February 2013

At 16, I was preoccupied with boys. And acting. I was a very lucky 16-year-old. I was born in a council estate in Tottenham but got a scholarship to grammar school, where I could have drama lessons. My school saved my life, I adored it. I simply wouldn't have lasted at a comprehensive, I was too easily knocked out of the way. The war had just finished, all my family had been in it, cousins had been killed – but lots of my male teachers were soldiers who'd just fought and they were very idealistic. My parents wanted me to leave at 14, they were furious I wasn't leaving to go and earn money like my brother and sister had. They wanted me to be a chorus girl. That's what they saw me doing because I'd been a performer all my life and that's what I'd trained to do. But a teacher convinced them to let me stay till I was 16, when I could hopefully go to drama school. And that's what I did, which was terrifically lucky. Though I was very sad that I couldn't stay till I was 18.

My mother was very superstitious. She sent me to dance lessons when I was very young because a gypsy woman came to our door and predicted that I would be a famous dancer. The awful thing was, I turned out to be a very good dancer so my mother thought it was all working out wonderfully. But I hated it. I had to work in working men's clubs two or three times a week. I was exhausted most of the time. When I was 12, I had a fantastic row at home and said I wasn't doing it any more. My teachers found out I was doing it around then, and that I was being pressured at home and by the time I was 13, I'd stopped. But what I hated, I did very cheap dancing, the kind that got you out of the working classes. I knew from a young age that there was something wrong with a little girl being told to dance on a table singing saucy songs and told to lift up her skirt. I didn't know the word then. Now I know it's paedophilia. But my parents didn't see anything wrong with it. One of their friends, who was a vicar, saw me do it at a party when I was seven, a Carmen Miranda number, a come-on. I rattled my non-existent tits, and he said to my mother, this is wrong.

I didn't feel comfortable at drama school but I was so completely passionate about acting, as I still am, that I put up with everything else. I cheated a bit – the only way I could get a grant was to say I'd be a teacher so I had to do that, which was very hard work and made for very long days. What was awful was that of all the girls at drama school I was the only female who went on to become an actress. Most of them were really going as a kind of finishing school. They were much richer than me. I met a boy who had done national service, a few years older than me, who went home the same way as me at night. He was the only boy I had anything in common with so we immediately became engaged.

I began elocution lessons when I was about nine – my dancing teacher suggested them, and she gave me them herself. They were appalling, my mouth was twisted this way and that. I never liked her. When I was in panto at 12 I had six lines and my mother was terribly proud. But one night after the show some woman came into the dressing room and said, 'Oh, I loved the little cockney.' My mother was absolutely appalled, so she asked the school to get rid of my cockney accent. And that's how I met this amazing man who offered to teach me for nothing. I owe my life to him, he was an extraordinary man. I didn't know at the time but he actually fancied me. The other teachers all knew, they used to keep a guard outside the classroom to make sure I was okay. He was 32 and I was 12. It never entered my head that an old man would be interested in me but actually in the end he married a woman even younger than me. The story ended up in the *News of the World* – she got an amazing splashy divorce to marry him. He was a defrocked priest who built a chapel in his basement and it turned out he could only fuck her if she got on the altar.

I was a very confident, social child because I was so adored by my mother. My parents had a loveless marriage. My father was a lovely cockney bloke who'd adored his first wife. But he lost her and was left with a child and he moved into our house and asked my mother if she'd help him look after the child. My mother was 39 and thought she was plain and would never marry. So she agreed to help, but only if he married her. After they married my mother had two boys straight away. Then she got pregnant again, had the child aborted and around the same time, one of her sons got meningitis and died. So she thought God had punished her for the abortion. One day my parents had a fantastic row. My father had just had an operation and my mother was telling him he wasn't a man anymore, and my father knocked my mother down and fucked her on the floor and the result was me. My mother thought God, had forgiven her and given her the girl she'd always wanted. So I was very loved.

I've always felt sexy. I've got a theory about who's sexy and who's not. I had a row the other day with a friend of mine who thought that Keira Knightley was the most beautiful thing he'd ever seen. And I said, but she's not sexy at all! I have this theory that if you like sex and you're confident, there's no reason why you shouldn't be sexy. I think most people who really like sex are attractive. A lot of very beautiful people are told they're beautiful when they're young and they think that's all they have to be. So they don't develop – they don't think they have to be funny or witty in a conversation, they don't think they have to be entertaining, they just think, well I'm beautiful, you're very lucky to have me on your arm. And some men are so bloody stupid they're happy with that, they think it gives them kudos. Good luck to them, they'll have a boring night. But most interesting men want an interesting woman. If you're bothering all the time about how you look, you're going to be boring. I think pure beauty is very boring, I don't like it in either sex. And often I've found it means the person will be very dull too.

I like rough, naughty-looking men, wicked men who look like they're up to no good. And Colin Farrell is one of those. (Eileen made headlines for spurning Farrell's advances when she was 70 and he was 28.) When I went to make the film with

Colin Farrell (*Ask the Dust*, 2006) I said no to the movie, the money wasn't very good and it wasn't a great part. And I was told, but Colin has asked specially for you. And I said, who's Colin? So he sent me a copy of the film *Phone Booth*. I looked at it and thought, my God, he's a good actor and he is a wildly attractive young man.

I was very unhappy when I was doing the last series of *Upstairs, Downstairs* (the long-running TV series in which she starred and also co-created). I didn't like the character; I didn't want to be an upstairs character, all the interesting ones are downstairs. I agreed to do a *Radio Times* interview but I had to fight very hard not to have this publicity 'minder' in the room. I refused to speak unless he left. These people make actors absolute puppets. I've been told that next to my name on a few companies' list it says 'loose cannon'. I probably shouldn't say the things I say. But then again, why is there this control everywhere? Actors are afraid to say anything.

If I met my younger self now I'd think, my God, what a little show-off. I think I'd find myself amusing but I'd also think her a little madam. But if you want to get out of the working classes – and in those days you had to if you wanted to be an actor – you probably have to be. If I told her how things were going to be for her – well, I've been one of the luckiest people on God's earth. I only wanted to be a repertory actress, I didn't want to be famous, but I've been allowed to be exactly the kind of actress I would have dreamed of being. I'm afraid of sounding smug but I couldn't have had a better life. Imagine telling that young girl she would be a dame! That she would play Saint Joan at 43. Or work with people like Michael Gambon or Alan Bates!

I'd love to tell that 16-year-old Tottenham girl that one

day she'll be presented with an honorary doctorate from Oxford University. I'm about to start crying just thinking of it. I wish I'd been clever enough to go somewhere like Oxford. The fact I was given that honour was beyond belief. It was such a beautiful day. We stayed in the college itself, in the Bishop's bedroom, and it was so lovely. They gave us lunch and dinner and the whole experience was sheer magic. I was extremely honoured when I got my damehood as well. Prince Charles told me I'd done a 'wonderful curtsey' so I felt very pleased with myself.

Caroline Lucas

Former Green Party Leader
6 April 2015

As a teenager I had my head in a book most of the time. My best friend was from a very literary family, and she was always bringing in poetry books or novels which we would hide away and read when we were supposed to be studying or doing sports, which neither of us much liked. There were very few books in my house so meeting her was a life-changing process. I would never have come across the likes of Emily Dickinson, for example, if I hadn't met her.

My parents were very reserved. Not uncaring, but that's just the way they were. My dad ran a small business and my mum brought up three kids. I guess it was a very practical family. My dad spent most of his weekends tinkering with the car. My mother would be baking. My siblings were older than me, so they weren't there for my teenage years. It felt more like being an only child. I didn't like that so much.

I would have liked more noise and hubbub and the feeling that something was going on. It was a quiet house.

I'd like to go back and tell my teenage self to relax, you're okay. I was always a terrible worrier; I bit my fingernails to the bone. There's a family story that when I was very little I left a tap on in the house and we went out and the house was in a bad state when we got back. That has always stayed with me, that worry that I've done something I didn't mean to and there will be consequences.

I think I was quite driven at 16. I wanted to do well at school. I wanted to be a rebel and a troublemaker but I also wanted to get good qualifications. It was quite a strict school so I deliberately broke the rules, going off at lunchtimes in my much-older boyfriend's car. My father was utterly frustrated by my decision to study English at university. He wanted me to learn German and do something practical. But I didn't worry, or even think much, about jobs, security, that kind of thing. That seemed to be a dreary thought. For me, life was for the living, and about devouring experience through books.

If you told the teenage Caroline she'd go into politics she'd think that was extraordinary – how on earth did that happen? She wasn't political at all. The idea of standing up for something you believe in though, if I'd thought about that properly, I'd have thought it was a wonderful thing to do.

I suppose now I think about it, that thing I had about rebelling but still getting my homework done – you could make a connection between that and something like getting arrested for protesting against fracking (for which she was charged but found not guilty in 2013). But by then it wasn't just about the rebelling, it was about being able to make a convincing case about why fracking was wrong and making a speech about that in Parliament. I felt it was incredibly important to be able to do that, not just be someone who had broken the law but couldn't give a good account of why.

I think the younger me would be impressed that I'd tried to do things differently in politics, tried to show you don't need to be a white man in a grey suit. Even something as small as wearing a 'No More Page 3' t-shirt in the House of Commons (for which she was officially reprimanded two years ago). You can see a link there with who I was before. This institution with these ridiculous rules – pictures of Page 3 are perfectly acceptable to be shown in the Parliamentary estate but wearing a t-shirt saying 'No More Page 3' is unacceptable.

If I could go back to any time I'd go to when my youngest son was tiny and say no to a big job I took. I was working at Oxfam and I was offered this secondment to the Department of International Development. It meant a lot of travelling up to London and I regret taking it now. I wish I'd realised how quickly that time when your kids are very young goes. It's so precious. There will be plenty of chances to do those other things that seem so important. But having that incredibly special time with your kids – that will never come again.

I get incredibly nervous before I do *Question Time* (a weekly political TV panel show). I find it a terrifying experience and literally wake up for days before thinking about the most terrible question that I don't know how to answer. You torture yourself with these things. I think *Question Time* is in a category of its own when it comes to the horrors it holds. But when you are standing in Parliament and you know what you're talking about and people are listening, that is a great feeling.

It was never just about the environment for me. I was

very involved in the campaign for nuclear disarmament, the women's movement, and environmental issues. I felt like I was being pulled three ways. Then in 1986 I read Jonathon Porritt's book *Seeing Green* (published 1984) and he put all of those issues together into one coherent whole. It was a lightbulb moment. The Green Party isn't just about the environment, it's about the crucial link between environmental justice and social justice. It's lazy journalism and making leaps based entirely on our name which puts us in a much narrower box.

If someone had told me when I joined the Party in 1986 that we'd still only have one MP by 2015 I'd be pretty surprised. I really felt once we got the message out it would spark imaginations all over the country and our rise would be much faster. I've often felt frustrated by how hard it's been to get access to the media. There was no doubt that David Cameron's recent sudden championing of our right to be included in the TV political debates suited his narrative very well, but it did help us get a foot in the door.

If I could go back and relive any day, it would be my wedding. I spent too much of it worrying that it would all go to plan. It was an extraordinarily wonderful summer's day, with an African band playing music that everyone from the smallest child to the oldest granny was up dancing to. I love dancing, and this was the happiest music you can think of. It was such a happy day, idyllic actually, with everyone I wanted to be there. I'd love to go back and take it all in without the worry and distraction.

Viv Albertine

Musician, singer and writer
20 February 2019

At 16, I was at a comprehensive school in North London. I had long hair, parted in the middle, probably with peroxide slathered into it. Very dark eyebrows. No make-up. I had lots of friends whose parents were in the Communist Party so we were going to see alternative films, reading alternative books – I was a big reader. We were very poor, a one-parent family living in council accommodation, but what was good about that time was that I was able to get a very good alternative education. Maybe because I was always in the art department at school, that's probably where I found most of my mentors.

That alternative education stopped me going down that prescribed route you can take when you're poor, of being frightened of the arts and of taking risks. I went to art school when I was 17, confident that I was going to have an interesting life, even though I never had money. I still think that art education has served me well all through my life. It taught me how to look at life from a different angle, encouraged me to take weird routes, think creatively, take risks and not worry too much about failing. And now I'm old, creative thinking is fucking coming back into play, I can tell you.

I got on well with my mum when I was a teenager. I was out pretty much all the time, going to gigs or films. I was so much sociable than I am now. And Mum was pretty hands-off, she gave me an incredible amount of freedom. She knew I was living a life she could never have lived when she was a working-class teenager. She taught me to ask, how can I make my life interesting, not the usual 9 to 5? She was always encouraging me to think for myself, question authority, and that made me a very antagonistic, unusual young woman. Underneath there was real self-doubt and terrible fear – there still is – but I've worked my whole life not to let that dominate me.

By the time I was 13 I'd seen lots of bands live, everything from Bowie and T-Rex to weird jazz. When I went to university, I saw one of the Sex Pistols' first gigs. Then I bumped into Sid Vicious and Johnny Rotten on Portobello Road and told them I was going to buy an electric guitar. And Sid said okay, I'll be in a band with you. So he went off and got hold of a saxophone and we started meeting up in some squat. That folded after a few months and then I went to see The Slits play their first gig. And I had never seen anything like them in my life. They were just brilliant. So I rang them up. It was such a tiny scene, but everyone was trying to do something interesting, though most of us couldn't sing or play an instrument. It doesn't matter if you can't play if you've got something to say, that was what we always said.

If someone had told that shy, frightened little Viv that one day she'd be in a real band and writing well-received books, she'd say, you've made a mistake. That was a life for intellectual men with wide educations, enormous talent and all the right contacts. Can you see how impossible that would seem to her? That would have been the life of my dreams. And when I'm grumping off to do something I don't want to do, I should probably remind myself of that a bit more.

If I could take the 16-year-old Viv anywhere it would be to an open-air gig The Slits played at Alexandra Palace. That's a venue I'd gone to lots of times as a child with my mum, and then to see gigs. I went there to roller skate, have a snog behind the toilets. So to take her back there to this great big open-air concert, I think that was one of the pinnacles. But there have been a few of those – going to America, writing books and having them so well received. Being shortlisted for the Costa prize. I mean honestly, when you think of everything I've done, it sounds pretty good.

Do you know, the whole Slits experience was pretty dreadful? I was the one who worked hard and tried to make the others work. It was fucking exhausting and I ended up in hospital. Thank God my mum was there to say, they're treating you like shit. It still hurts me to this day. What I would say to the young me is, don't worry, Viv, in 30 or 40 years' time you'll still be that person having ideas and having the drive, writing books, making albums, writing new songs instead of just playing the old ones again and again. I know it's not cool to talk about that sort of thing but really, I've had enough. It's still painful to me. Why not talk honestly about it?

When you have a life-threatening illness (Viv was given a cervical cancer diagnosis six weeks after she gave birth to her daughter Vida) it's almost like you're drowning. You are so in the moment, fighting each thing as it comes. I was floored.

I had just had a baby, it was right up in my face. But if I hadn't had my baby I might have gone under completely. Someone did come and cook a meal for my husband and my child every night without being asked. I think it's great when someone does that without being asked because I didn't ask for help much. I went to ground, like an injured animal hiding in a hedge, licking my wounds. It took me years to get over it.

The cancer has fucked me a bit physically though it's not obvious when you look at me. The treatment is so brutal it does ruin your insides a bit. But I still duck and dive, even though I'm older and not as strong. In some ways this period of my life might be my best. I'm financially solvent, I have enough to buy a house, I can buy food. I've hassled and hustled and I've been put down a lot for not being very ladylike. But I wouldn't be the survivor I am if I had been fucking ladylike the whole time.

After doing all that work with The Slits and being exhausted by it for years, I did think, okay, Viv, you've done your bit now. Let the young girls come in and take the flame. But when I got my energy back after the cancer I was absolutely overwhelmed by the drive to do something new. Now I look back and feel very glad that I wrote the books. I think older people have so much to give if they are given more space to express themselves. I grew up dreading being old. I grew up in the Western world, where being old was just the pits. You were nothing, you were worthless, you were invisible. But I'm here to say the world is still all out there to be used and being old can completely and utterly be the best laugh ever.

Chapter 11:

Transformation

Dolly Parton

Singer-songwriter and philanthropist
19 October 2020

I actually was a pretty good girl at 16. I was in high school at the time, but I had been taking my music very seriously for several years before that, taking trips back and forth to Nashville with my Uncle Bill Owens, from my home in East Tennessee, 200 miles away. We'd take some old car, and sleep in the car, trying to go into different offices in Nashville. We'd stay a few days to try to get a few things going. I didn't have time to run around and mess with boys. And my dad was pretty strict anyway, so I pretty much spent my teenage years just working on my music and hanging out with friends when I had an opportunity.

I was about 13 when I first met Johnny (Cash) and that's when Johnny was all strung out on drugs and everything, but he was so magnetic, so sexy. He was my first male grown-up crush, he just really moved me. That's when I realised what hormones do and what sex appeal really means. He just kind

241

of stirred me somehow. And so I guess that's when I realised I was becoming a little woman. Oh, we laughed about it through the years. I told him, you know you were my very first crush, my first sexy grown-up crush. He always got a kick out of that.

I knew I wanted to always stay true to my roots. I knew I loved my family – I would never shame them, I was proud of my family. But I just had a feeling inside my gut that I was supposed to do something more. I felt it in my bones early on, it was just like a calling. I wanted to go beyond the Smoky Mountains. My family knew that as well, even though it was a little different for a low mountain girl.

I'm very proud of the fact that I'm so much both of my parents. I can see it so plain in myself. I got my spiritual side and my musical side from my mom's people. Most of them played musical instruments and sang, and we all grew up in the church. We were the family that played at funerals and weddings and all kinds of shindigs. My dad's people were mainly hard-working people; I got his work ethic and willingness to stick to it until I get the job done. I know what part of me is Daddy and I know which part is Mama and I think it's a good combination. It's why I've lasted so long. Usually creative musicians are basically kind of physically lazy. They want to stay up all night and write and sing and sleep all day. But like my dad, I get up really early, I work hard and I go to bed fairly early. And I love the fact that I'm not a lazy head, I'm not sluggish. I think that's been a big part of my success – I'm up and at it before most people can get out of bed.

My mom and dad were both very proud of me. My mom was more lenient in the early days, she used to have to cover for me. My dad didn't want me travelling – traipsing around, as he called it – he didn't like me going away to Nashville. He and my mom used to have words about that. So I'd go before he got home from work and Mama had to defend me on that one. She'd say, she's alright, and she's gonna leave whether you like it or not. Mama understood it because she was a dreamer also. But he was pretty strict, I thought sometimes in the early days he was too strict. It's not that he didn't trust me, he just didn't trust the world. But after I moved to Nashville he saw that I was serious about it and it was real work, and a dream that was actually possible. And he became my biggest fan and biggest supporter.

I always knew my ambition was going to happen, they couldn't preach it out of me. I was going to be a star, I was going to go to Nashville, I was going to sing my songs no matter what. I was never a rebel without a cause, I was not a rebellious child. I did it with grace and style. I wasn't out to cause any grief at all for my mom or dad, but I was willing to take whatever punishment I might have got for going against somebody's ruling. I am strong in my beliefs. There is an old saying, 'to thine own self be true'. That has followed me all the days of my life. I know who I am. I know what I'm not. I know what I can and cannot do. I don't get myself involved in things that I know are out of my realm. But if there's something I can do and I want to do, hell or high water ain't gonna stop me. I'm an easy person to work with, but I will not bend to your ways if they go against mine. I have my standards and my principles and if you push me to a point that does not agree with my soul, I will call you on it, and I will not compromise. I don't feel like I have to answer to anyone but myself and to God. That's my rule.

It's true I would not compromise with Colonel Tom (Elvis

Presley's manager). Elvis wanted to record 'I Will Always Love You' (originally written and recorded by Dolly in 1973). They planned the session and told me they were recording the song. I'd been invited down to the studio to meet Elvis and be there when he sang my song. That was the most exciting thing that had ever happened to me. Who doesn't love Elvis? But then Colonel called me the afternoon before the session and said, 'You do know we have to have at least half the publishing on any song that Elvis records?' And I said, 'No, I did not know that.' He said, 'Well, it's just a rule.' So I said, 'Well, it's not my rule … I hate this more than you could even imagine but I cannot give you half the publishing. I just can't do it and I won't do it.' 'I Will Always Love You' had been a number one song with me already, it was the most important song in my catalogue. And I cried all night long, 'cause I was so disappointed. It wasn't Elvis, I loved Elvis. And I'm sure he was as disappointed as I was because he had it all worked up and ready to go.

I know he loved the song. Priscilla told me later that he sang that song to her when they were coming down the steps of the courthouse after they divorced. That really touched me and I thought, oh well, I can only imagine. But it wasn't his fault. I found out later that Colonel Tom had an even bigger demand for any brand new song Elvis recorded; in those cases 100 per cent of the publishing went to them. Tom was a strict manager, he was a good manager and I don't blame him for asking, but I don't blame me for saying no.

When you write songs you don't know what's going to be a hit. As a songwriter you know when some songs are better than others and I knew that 'I Will Always Love You' was probably one of the best things that I'd written, because it came from so much heart and soul. But you never know what's going to be a hit or everybody would be rich. I knew it was a good song but I had no idea that it could ever become what it did, after Whitney recorded it and it went into such a big hit movie (*The Bodyguard*, released in 1992). I'll always be grateful to Kevin Costner and obviously I'll always be grateful to and always love Whitney Houston.

'Jolene' and 'I Will Always Love You' were on the same album around 1972. In fact, they came from the same cassette so it is possible that I wrote those two songs in the same day. 'Jolene' is a song about... you know, I've got my pride and I've got my strength. But when I write a song, I'm vulnerable at those moments. I leave my heart out on my sleeve. I've always said I have to leave my heart open in order to receive those kind of songs. I have to feel everything to be a real songwriter. And yes, a lot of my songs are kind of melancholy. Some of them are sad, and some of them are pitiful. And I mean for them to be pitiful, those really sad songs like 'Little Sparrow' or 'Jeannie's Afraid of the Dark'. I have a big imagination and I become whoever I'm writing about. It's like starring in a movie; I am that character in that song. So when I wrote it, I was Jolene.

'Jolene' has been recorded more than any other song that I have ever written. It has been recorded worldwide over 400 times in lots of different languages, by lots of different bands. The White Stripes did a wonderful job of it, and many other people. But nobody's ever had a really big hit record on it. I've always hoped somebody might do someday, someone like Beyoncé.

What I would say to my young self is all those dreams, they are going to come true. It's not going to all be fun and games, you're going to have to pay the price and do your sacrificing, but it's going to be worth it. I'd have to tell her about 'I Will Always Love You'. To me that is really a classic love song. I had a number one on it twice, once in '72, then I did it in the movie *Best Little Whorehouse in Texas* and had another number one. Which is the first time the same song has ever been number one with the same artist. And then Whitney did it and it was considered one of the greatest love songs of all time. Still to this day I take a lot of pride in that. So I'd tell my younger self, you're going to end up being very proud of your little old self one day. So just buckle up and be ready for the ride.

If I could have one last conversation with anybody, I'd probably talk to Elvis. And I'd probably talk about 'I Will Always Love You' and say hey, I bet you were as disappointed as I was about all that and I still dream about you singing that song. Matter of fact, I even wrote a song called 'I Dreamed about Elvis Last Night' and I had an Elvis soundalike sing it with me and we actually sing 'I will always love you' in it. And one day, I'm going to put that track out. So I think that I'd talk to Elvis, and just clear that up with him.

If I could live one moment of my life again, I think it's when I became an official member of the Grand Ole Opry, back in the late '60s. When I found out it was going to happen I jumped up and down, I was tickled to bits. I had always wanted to be on the Grand Ole Opry (the legendary weekly country music show in Nashville). You would listen to it on the radio back home and hear all those singers and that was where you wanted to be if you were a country singer. I remember that night so well. I remember how proud I felt thinking of my people listening back home. That memory stands out the most because that was the very first big moment. But I've had many, many special nights since then.

Jenny Agutter

Actress

20 August 2012

By the time I was 16 I was at ballet school and already making films. I'd just made *Walkabout* (released 1971) in Australia and was about to make *The Railway Children* (released 1970). I didn't think at all about the future. I knew I enjoyed acting but at 16, I had no life experience; the characters I was playing were really just who I was, a child. (Directors) Nick Roeg and Lionel Jeffries just used that extraordinarily well. They were very honest performances in that sense.

My parents were away in Cyprus while I was at boarding school. I didn't see them very much. They weren't particularly impressed or over-awed by the whole film thing, they just let me get on. It's a peculiar situation, who knows what it does to you – these are the people you love most, who are the closest people to you, but you hardly see them and when you do it takes a week for you all to get used to each other again. The closest I was to my mother before she died was when my son was born years later; I began to appreciate what she'd done for me and she absolutely adored my son.

If I could talk to that girl now I'd say don't give up your education at 17. I think an education would have given me confidence, more choices, and helped me focus my thoughts when I try to explain what I mean. It made me self-conscious in my twenties – I was thrown into work alongside people who were highly educated and I felt I didn't know what they were talking about. Now I'd tell that younger me, people are very willing to tell you things; you can find out a lot if you just ask and listen. But I thought I'd look foolish if I asked questions.

With acting you never lose that sense of never quite knowing how much longer it can continue. At 14, I was told acting was all very well but it was likely to dry up soon. So I've never taken it too seriously. When I was 21, and working at the National Theatre, Peter Hall gave me very good advice – to go around the repertory theatres, do some Shakespeare, really work on my craft. I didn't listen to him, of course. I went to make movies in LA.

I'd tell my younger self she has a hell of a lot going for her at an unusually early age, and she should make more of it. When I went to LA, I did all those stupid photo shoots, sitting in a bathing costume with your hair down your back and lots of make-up on. Pretty vacuous stuff and it had nothing to do with getting good roles. I should have felt more confident about the weight of work I already had behind me and just said no.

In terms of relationships, I clearly wasn't pursuing settling down or having a family in my twenties. I must have backed off for some reason. I was aware during the sixties it was a burgeoning, liberated time, but my childish side was still very strong, and in a way I was still thinking like the Little Mermaid. I was still giving up my tail and getting legs and finding it all rather painful. If I could go back now I'd tell myself, you don't have to be the Little Mermaid, you can experiment; it can actually be rather fun.

The reason I married so late was that I didn't really grow up until my late thirties. I think that was because of my crazy adolescence, spending time with all these grown-ups but being afraid of asking questions. They seemed to assume I had all this maturity but emotionally, I really wasn't mature at all. I knew I couldn't have children on my own, that would never have been my choice. I had my son when I was 37, when I was ready for all that, and I'm really glad I had a partner to see me through it all.

What a surprise at my age that I've never been busier. The success of *Call the Midwife* (the popular TV drama that has been running since 2012) has been extraordinary and such a lovely surprise. I've been stopped in the street in a way I never have been before. But it is daunting, getting older. Men are still called attractive when they're 80, but if you suggest a woman of that age is attractive people say, what do you mean by that? It's always a surprise to me to see that I look older when I look in the mirror. And now I have contact lenses I can see all my wrinkles. But inside I still feel 35.

Emmylou Harris

Singer-songwriter

23 July 2021

I had just gotten into folk music when I was 16. I got a guitar, and I was learning everything I could, which basically ended up being three chords. There was a radio station in Washington DC, about 25 miles away, which played folk music every night. It opened up a whole world for me, all these songs and incredible singers and songwriters. I had my radio on every night while I was doing my homework, just discovering all these artists like Joan Baez, who was really the one who made me pick up a guitar. Besides her music, I feel she changed the heart of America through her involvement in the civil rights movement, using her voice, literally using her voice, the way she did. I'd love to tell that teenage girl listening to the radio that one day she'll be onstage singing for Joan Baez at her induction into the Kennedy Center Honors (in June 2021).

Looking back on the 16-year-old me, I feel a certain

tenderness towards that young girl. I didn't know much, I was very naive. I had a very sheltered life. I was very intense. I would say to that girl, try to have more fun. I worried about getting good grades. I didn't really know how to flirt. I didn't date. I didn't really know how to fit into the social fabric of high school. And I didn't see how I could have a career in music because I didn't study music, I didn't know music theory. So I thought music would just be something I would do on the side.

I was 21 when I moved to New York City. That's pretty young, I guess. I didn't know anyone except the wonderful singer-songwriter Paul Siebel, who introduced me to David Bromberg and Jerry Jeff Walker and all the people who were making music in the (Greenwich) Village. It was a very creative time. I started making music with friends, trying to get little gigs, learning my craft. I was very inspired by the people I heard play, like Joni Mitchell and Townes Van Zandt – I was quite astounded the first time I saw him. I never imagined I would end up recording (the Van Zandt penned) 'Pancho and Lefty', which became a real central part of my repertoire.

I had the most extraordinarily loving parents. We were a very close family and I had a wonderful upbringing in Virginia. Then one day I just kind of said to them, right, I'm out of here. I'm going to New York. And looking back now, as a parent, I just really can't believe I put them through that. But they knew I had to follow my own course. They couldn't have been more supportive, because when I got up there, I ended up getting married (to songwriter Tom Slocum) and having my first daughter (when she was 22), and then my marriage broke up a year later. I went back home with my daughter and it was always a safe haven. It was like, everything's okay, you have a home as long as you want it. There was never any judgement or anything like that.

I think my parents were probably convinced they could stop worrying about me when my first record (1969's *Gliding Bird*) came out. All of a sudden your daughter's got her picture on an album cover! They were proud and I think they were also relieved. I actually dedicated that record to them. Over time they got to know all my band members; when we played in the area, we would always go to visit them. And we would have a little football game in the front yard and they would have a barbecue for everyone. My parents became part of the whole deal.

I really believe no one would have paid me any attention if it wasn't for Gram (Parsons, with whom she made the two seminal albums, *GP* and *Grievous Angel*). When I met him, I had not found my own voice. I was an imitator; you have to start that way. But I really do believe that it was Gram who gave me not just my voice but he taught me about understanding music and feeling music, the way it came through me. Of course, I certainly had something to build on. But he was that last rocket boost, and after that everything kind of fell into place.

I'd like to tell my younger self that though it will be very difficult when Gram dies (in 1973, aged 26), it will be okay again eventually. That was a very hard time because I really felt I had found where I was supposed to be. Even though I probably assumed that at some point I would make a record on my own, that was something I wasn't even thinking about. I just was thinking about what we would do together. Musically, I mean. Then suddenly I'd lost a friend and a teacher, someone I felt I still had so much to learn from. It was devastating. But I had wonderful support from my family and my musical friends, and they helped me take one step at a time. I was nourished and I gathered strength and was able to move forward.

If I could go back to my younger self, especially in the most difficult times, I would just say, don't worry. Just do what you feel in your heart and everything will be alright. Because it always did turn out okay. There was a time when I went into deep debt over a project, *The Ballad of Sally Rose* (a self-penned album based loosely on her relationship with Gram Parsons, previously described by Harris as 'a commercial disaster'). But I don't have any regrets about doing it at all because it was real creative reclaiming. After that I had to work my way back up but then, all of a sudden, I did this record called *Trio* with Linda Ronstadt and Dolly Parton (a multi-million seller in 1987 and the biggest success of her career). So the creative chances always seemed to come along. Certainly, there were times when it seemed like I was treading water. But I didn't really have any other talents, the only thing I knew how to do was sing. So in a sense I had no choice.

If I could spend time with anyone just one more time it would be my father. He died very suddenly and I was not there. My mother ended up coming to live with me, and she lived with me for 21 years. My parents were so close, they were almost like one entity. In the 21 years that my mother lived with me we became the greatest friends. Of course we'd always loved each other but now we travelled together, we did many things together and I got to know her as a person. But with my father, I never got that chance, even though he was an extraordinary influence on me. He was my hero. He was a war hero (Marine Corps officer Walter Harris spent ten months as a prisoner of war during the Korean War), but he was also my hero as a father, as a husband, as a brother, as a neighbour.

I wish I could have told him a lot of things. He knew I loved him but there were conversations that I wish we could have had. I wish I'd spent more time with him, maybe under the hood of a car – he was a great mechanic. He was also a wonderful gardener. They're the wonderful gifts he had, that I wish I could have shared with him more. I wish I could tell him how much he meant to me, even though I think he knew.

If I could live one day again it would be when my second daughter was born. With my first one, I didn't really know much about babies or being a mother. And I suppose my life was still a little rocky at that point. But with my second daughter, my husband (producer Brian Ahern) and I had a great relationship. We both already had daughters from other marriages and having a child together was a sort of combination of our love and respect and regard for each other, and the life we were going to have becoming a family with the other daughters. At that point, the world was in a perfect place and all the planets were aligned.

Rosamund Pike

Actor

21 November 2016

At 16, I'd just had the best summer of my life because I'd just joined the National Youth Theatre. I found my tribe. I never felt I fitted in very well, then I found these people from all over the country, all different backgrounds, united by passion. I think I gave the illusion of being quite a happy teenager but inside I'd been craving to find that passion. Until then I was surrounded by this idea that it was cool not to care too much, or try too hard.

I got a scholarship to go to school and my parents said, you're going to be around a lot of people who are a lot better off than we are. Hold your head up high. They drove me in to sit my exam and the exhaust pipe fell off our old car at the school gates. The whole time I was doing the exam I could see my mum in front of the car with the bonnet up. And all these other parents were cruising in with very modern cars. I remember people talking about jet lag and thinking, what on earth are they talking about? I didn't experience jet lag until I was in my twenties and I got the Bond film and had to fly to LA. That was my first trip to America and suddenly it was first class travel, cars to the airport. It was the magic carpet ride.

If you grew up without money, your attitude to it never changes, no matter how well off you are. So I will still get in a cab and think, my God, it's £8. Even though I can afford that now, I still feel that rising panic as I watch the meter go up.

When I was growing up and going to parties I was not the girl boys were interested in. That's the truth. But it didn't bother me too much. I don't think I was ready for boys. I just watched other girls and thought, maybe that'll be me some day. I remember one day at the Youth Theatre I was going up the stairs and this boy I knew shouted 'Hi gorgeous!' I looked around, I had no idea he was talking to me. I probably did change a bit when that happened. But inside, I can still see that awkward girl covering her embarrassingly rosy cheeks with corrective green make-up.

I was rejected from a number of drama schools before I went to university. It was devastating at the time. But I knew what I was. I was an actress and they could knock me down but they couldn't knock that out of me. I suppose it made me feel I want to prove them wrong. I made a film with Christian Bale over the summer and he told me he didn't go to drama school either. I thought here I am, sitting next to one of the greatest actors in the world and neither of us went to drama school. I thought back to all those people who rejected me and thought, well there you are, I've shown you wrong. Or maybe not – maybe they're sitting thinking, why on earth is she getting all those roles, she's shit. But they never managed to crush me.

That sudden change of life – being in a Bond film, flying first class – it can make you feel giddy. You feel shaky because the ground isn't solid any more. I remember afterwards I got a play at the Royal Court and I was on the 137 bus going over Chelsea Bridge. And I was thinking, thank God, I know how to do this. I know how to take the bus, go to a grubby rehearsal room, eat my sandwich. I felt very rooted again. The magic carpet is great but you have to know you'll come back down to earth again. I still get that feeling.

I would really contest the idea that I've had this rocky road love life (as diagnosed by *The Daily Mail*). I think I've had a pretty normal road. Most people are heartbroken at some point in their lives (Pike's fiancé, director Joe Wright, pulled out of the wedding with just weeks to go). I was about 28 when my marriage was called off and I remember all my friends gathering around, inviting me to things – but they were all in couples. It was so hard. I remember feeling that I couldn't face Christmas because it was all about family and I felt so alone.

I was madly in love with people who hurt me. But I'm happy now. And I wouldn't change anything even if I could. I'd still love the people I've loved. You have to live. Love is always a risk. God, if you could fast-forward me from that sad time and say, in a few years you'll have two little boys and you'll have this amazing family, it's going to be okay. It makes me feel a bit teary now to think of it. A few years ago my agent gave me two dog tags with my sons' names on. I remember sitting on my own in LA – I'd just been nominated for an Oscar – not long after I'd given birth to my second son. And I was looking at these dog tags thinking, my goodness, here is the fact of my two children, here are their names and their dates of birth. I made these people. It's extraordinary really.

Being a Bond girl was very intimidating. I remember when I was doing the play in London after that film, feeling I was letting everyone down because they weren't getting the Bond girl, they were just getting me. A huge letdown. But I did get over that, juggling the image on the screen with the real me. It occurred to me some people might prefer to see the real me, the imperfect me.

If I could tell my teenage self that some of the men who were posters on my wall... that I'd end up working with them! That I'd have Tom Cruise round for dinner. It's insane, right? In terms of recognition *Gone Girl* (the 2014 film for which she received an Oscar nomination) completely changed my life. I was in my local store recently buying nappies at night and the woman behind the till said, 'Oh my goodness, you look exactly like what's her name, you know the one, she was in that film with Ben Affleck.' The other teller nudged her and said, 'No, I think that is her.' And she said, 'Don't be daft, she's from Hollywood!'

If I could relive any time in my life it would be the moment when I went into my agent's office to look at some headshots I'd had done. And he was down in the lobby with his arms open and he said, 'Darling, you're the next Bond girl!' And I knew that taxi meter wasn't going to be so scary any more. But the best ever moment was when I heard the first cry of my first child and I felt like my heart – I'm going to cry now – I felt like it leapt across the room.

Peggy Seeger

Singer-songwriter
4 November 2019

I was intrigued by a lot of poetry as a teenager; I loved Shakespeare. My parents didn't have a lot of time to spend with us but the special thing my family brought to me was folk music. I started learning guitar when I was six, and the banjo when I was 15. And I played the piano quite well, though I didn't have the nerve to play for other people. But it was a long time before I started writing my own songs, not until I was 25. When I was a teenager I didn't think of doing music for a living. I liked it too much. As a job it seemed like very hard work.

There were four of us kids. My mother (Ruth Crawford Seeger, now regarded as one of the most important modernist composers of the century) was a piano teacher, my father was a music administrator. We lived in a large house in a very select area of Washington DC, which we couldn't afford and we often went into debt. My father was a Communist in the

'30s, though I didn't learn that until I was 35. My mother was a closet feminist, which she had to dampen down when she married my father. We never talked politics in the house. We had black women working in the house because my mother taught 12 hours a day. The black women did not sit down at the dinner table with us. When I had live-in help with my children in Beckenham everyone sat together for dinner. My father was intrigued by that when he came to visit.

My mother died of cancer when I was in my first year of college and my father had to retire because of McCarthyism. The family fell apart – my mother had been the love of my father's life. Everyone had to move to my college town and live in a tiny apartment, but there was no money for my education. Then my father fell in love and married again and he wasn't terribly keen on having his children around. He was a bit of a selfish man. So he decided I should go to Holland to live with my older brother. I didn't really get on with my stepmother but I think that was because I was a terrible teenager. She wasn't a bad person at all. If I could go back, I would apologise to her profusely.

I hitchhiked around Holland, then Belgium, where I was picked up by a Catholic priest. I lived with him in his tiny little village, looking after a group of displaced children he'd brought back from East Berlin. He tried to convert me. I was cold and depressed and overworked, and I almost converted until some friends came to visit, saw I was 'turning Catholic', kidnapped me and took me in their little Fiat to Denmark. That's where I was when Alan Lomax (the famous music 'field' recorder who had worked with her half-brother, Pete Seeger) tracked me down and took me to London to sing and play banjo on a TV show he was making. I was a scruffy tomboy then but just before he introduced me to his friends his model girlfriend re-dressed me; she did my hair into a beehive and put make-up and earrings and high heels on me. And I tottered into that room and met a group of musicians Alan had very knowingly brought together. And that's when I met (legendary folk singer-songwriter) Ewan MacColl.

Ewan MacColl fell head over heels in love with me. He chased me for three years. I thought he was funny-looking. And he was 20 years older than me, with a wife and child. And that was a no-no for me. But he tracked me down and two days later, we started an affair. His wife had already been unfaithful twice and he had been unfaithful too. She loved him though, the way he wanted to be loved. Which I didn't. I loved him but I wasn't mad about him. I wasn't intending to stay with him or marry him. In the end though, he was the right person for me, definitely; the father figure my father had never been. And he was very intelligent and fascinating to be with.

One of the first songs I wrote was 'I'm Gonna Be an Engineer'. After that women started asking me to perform other feminist songs so I had to start writing them! And I started researching the issues and became a radical feminist. The more I read, the more I realised how privileged I was. And how unequal my life at home with Ewan was. I did the shopping, the cooking, all that. After Ewan died, I got more and more passionate about ecology alongside feminism and I realised how much men had destroyed the earth. Women look after things. We don't take our sons out and dress them as soldiers. It's men who are violent. It's men who torture. It's men who rape, and kill, and go onto schoolyards with guns.

Joan Baez came for my autograph in 1961, at the Newport Festival. We've never had a proper conversation but I'd have loved to. I'd like to do a concert with her but she's too high-up for me. She's the folk goddess of America. Dylan wanted our autograph too, in Minnesota, when he was still a student wearing a tie and carrying a little briefcase. Two years later, when we went back to Minnesota, Bob Zimmerman had become Bob Dylan. And the promoter who'd brought us back said, remember that funny little guy who followed you around a couple of years ago... ?

If I could have one last conversation with anyone, it would be my mother. I would want to know more about her. When I hear her compositions I am completely blown away. Because the person I knew as my mother is not someone I thought could write anything like that. She had so many hopes and dreams that she wrote about when she was still in college. She was close to her own mother, she wrote to her every day when she was away at music school. But my mother never talked about her mother. She didn't talk about her. And I don't know that I talked about my mother to my children. Because I never really knew who she was. But now I talk to her in my head.

I've only been in love once in my life, and that was with my present partner, Irene Pyper-Scott. I don't think I was in love with Ewan. I loved him dearly but the head-over-heels love he had for me made me aware that I didn't love him the same way. But I love Irene in that way. That kind of love is dangerous. It's like an illness. To me it felt atomic. And it came at a very difficult point in my life. I fell in love with her before Ewan died; he was ill for the last ten years of his life. She was my best friend and I fell in love with her. Ewan and I were together for 30 wonderful years, and now Irene and I have been together for 30 years. Ewan MacColl made me who I was with him. But Irene Pyper-Scott made me who I am without anybody.

Chapter 12:

Ageing

Juliet Stevenson

Actor

23 May 2016

At 16, I really felt I was connecting to the world of ideas. It was around then English literature exploded in my head. I was listening to David Bowie and John Lennon, in the time of the four-day week, the Heath government, the huge polarising of the have and have nots – I became quite politicised. I learned about social injustice, power, privilege, moral responsibilities. I was really on a journey of connecting to the world. I remember that time viscerally, I can go straight back. We never lose an age, we carry them all in us our whole lives.

It was at 16 I saw my first Shakespeare play. Five actors in t-shirts and jeans came to our school and did a cutdown version of *King Lear*. I walked into the school hall one person and walked out a changed person. I was just astonished and enraptured by the play and the language. And I identified very strongly with King Lear. I've always puzzled over why a

16-year-old girl should identify so much with King Lear, but if you look at the play, he's volatile, loses his temper, he has a strong sense of injustice as he discovers poverty, a world that is very unequal. And he is racked by guilt about his own privilege. All those qualities are very teenage, really.

Looking back, I see myself as very gauche. I had two brothers but I'd been in boarding schools since I was nine due to my dad being in the army. So I was very socially unconfident about boys and all that. I was skinny, quite a late developer. I wasn't very comfortable in my body. I had secret loves but not many requited love affairs. I'd tell that teenager not to worry – quite soon you'll discover there's a world out there where it'll be okay to be yourself so just hang on in there. I'd also tell her, regarding her eyebrows – there is a point when you should stop plucking.

I never thought I'd be a movie star. You have to feel confident about the way you look to feel that. So when I made *Truly Madly Deeply* (released 1990) I thought, God, how amazing, to be on a 30-foot-high screen. Making that film gave me enormous confidence. It validated what I hoped would be true; that the integrity of the work will get you there. There's an awful lot of other stuff in our business – who you know, who you schmooze, how you look, all the social and sexual games I found confusing and didn't want to do. But with *Truly Madly Deeply* I worked with this close group of friends – Alan Rickman, Anthony Minghella, Michael Maloney – and made a film with integrity. And it opened up a lot of career doors for me.

I'd like to tell my younger self, you're going to be in a position to make a real difference one day. So much of my life has come as a surprise to me. Even when I was at drama school I didn't think I'd be a successful actress. I assumed I would be one of the unsuccessful ones. In my twenties I thought I'd been so lucky with my career I'd have to pay the price for that by not finding a man I'd want to settle down with, and not having the children that I craved. So to have a partner whom I adore – we've been 23 years together – with a bunch of children... Sometimes I feel, when the house is full of people and I'm cooking, God, isn't this amazing!

I don't think men have their trajectory interrupted very much, and women do. You have to work harder and harder against the sense that you're losing value as you get older. You're trying to protest against that value system, yet you also have to play the game a bit. I found turning 40 very difficult. I still struggle with being introduced as a 'veteran' actor, going to France and being a Madame instead of a Madamoiselle. I'd love to go back to my younger self and tell her it won't keep getting harder. In fact, it will become easier. I'm actually really enjoying my fifties, and I never thought I'd say that. I used to worry about what visual image I should project. Glamour was a long reach for me. Now I finally feel confident about myself – I can stand up and talk about what I believe in and be who I am and accept the fact I'm not going to please everyone.

My 16-year-old self would have disapproved of some of the work I've done. I try not to do rubbish, but you have to pay the mortgage. And some years there just aren't the scripts. Sometimes you do the big money projects to have the luxury of doing the interesting, challenging work at the Royal Court or the Old Vic for take-home pay of about £300 a week. I'm quite happy with that now – I've got children, I'm a breadwinner, I have to pay bills. But my teenage self would have been very judgemental.

I really loved my older brother, who died 15 years ago when I was expecting my youngest child. That's 15 years of lost conversations. If I could go back in time, I'd love to claim some of those back. And my dad died when I was 35. That's my big sadness, that he never knew my children. He would have loved to see the fine young adults they're growing into. He was a great appreciator. And I look at my brother's daughter, my much-loved niece, and her lovely young boy – he didn't know him either – and I think my dad would have taken such joy from him. But I talk to them both all the time in my head. My brother loved driving and whenever I'm going round in the car desperately looking for somewhere to park, and somebody pulls out to give me the perfect space in central London, I always say, 'Thanks, darling.'

If I could go back and have one more time in my life again, it would be about 16 years ago when we were all – my partner Hugh, and my son and daughter – in Australia. My daughter was six and my son was just born. I'd longed for a second child and I'd finally had him. I finished filming for the day and we all went for this amazing lunch. We were sitting on a tiny Chinese junk boat chugging out to the Great Barrier Reef, sun beating down, baby in a pouch on my chest, my six-year-old daughter swimming alongside the boat with porpoises swimming next to her. And I thought, oh my God, it couldn't get better than this. And I knew it at the time. I seized it. I sat on the deck of that boat with the sun and the sky and the sea, everyone in their element, and I thought, life couldn't be more fully lived than it is at this moment.

Debbie Harry

Singer-songwriter

13 May 2013

I was a typical 16-year-old, interested in the opposite sex, going to dances, gabbing on the phone to girlfriends. School was okay but it made me nervous. I was an achiever, a goal-orientated person, which has been a good thing in the long run, but I worried about getting good grades. I loved sports, softball and tennis. I was experimenting with different hair colours from an early age so I probably already had my bleached hair by 16. I was talking to a friend the other day, remembering that we started bleaching our hair from about 13. I told my parents my hair was getting lighter and lighter in the sun – I don't think I had it in mind to do anything outrageous but I wanted to look cool and sharp. Which meant a lot of fuss with my hair. I wore little skirts and sweaters, I don't think I had an extraordinary wardrobe. But I loved the movie stars, the sirens of the screen – Jane Fonda in *Barbarella*, Brigitte Bardot, and of course Marilyn.

Letter to My Younger Self: Inspirational Women

If I met my young self now, I'd think she was pretty quiet but a good listener. I was quite shy but I had a nice gang of girlfriends and I had boyfriends too. I think I was a fairly decent girlfriend. I didn't go around stomping on boys' hearts. I was a bit of a Walter Mitty. I had constant fantasies about the future, my rise to stardom. They didn't particularly involve being a pop singer, just a general idea that I would make it.

I have a lot of questions that I wish my younger self had asked my parents, questions only they could answer. I do have the feeling – wow, that was a really big miss. They came from a very different world, they weren't really part of modern culture. My mother loved opera. They were very conservative people, and they were very surprised by what I did but proud too. They kept a lot of cuttings.

It wasn't till I partnered up with Chris (Stein, her musical, and for 20 years, romantic partner) that I began to really believe something big could happen. I thought our combination of talents was unbeatable. We were at the bottom of the barrel in the clubs in New York but we inched our way up in a very zig-zag way, which may not have been the best way, to do business but it worked for us.

Being female gave me an edge in the CBGBs scene (a New York club known for giving a platform to American punk bands in the 1970s). There wasn't a lot of female competition though I knew it was going to come. There were a few of us but in general the music business did not have a lot of girls in it. The mystery of it all, I can't figure it out. I was criticised for being overtly feminine and exploiting my sexuality. To me that sounds like a weird paranoia because sexuality and rock'n'roll is the norm, it's always been that way. The only thing I was scared of was making sure it happened. You have to be pretty crazy and obsessed to make your living in a band, and that can lead to a certain blindness, a madness. But ultimately we were inspired because we felt something in the air. It was small, it wasn't a huge scene, but there was an immediacy about it and something was starting to happen.

At the time I was a little surprised about the attention, the focus I got in Blondie. I don't think everyone in the band was entirely happy with that, but I guess you have to ask them. We had to learn how the music business worked as we went along but sometimes it made it very awkward. I really wanted to be a good performer and get a good response from the audience and that propelled me and helped me deal with all the attention.

I'd tell my younger self that you need to make the first move with the audience. At the beginning I would go out onstage and expect the audience to respond. But gradually I figured out that I had to make it happen myself. There are a few instant prodigies, and they're wonderful, but the rest of us have to learn and practise, practise, practise to get good. I don't think I was ultimately a career person. I wanted to be an artist.

I took a lot of inspiration from the other bands in New York, watching how they put their shows together. Everyone had a very different approach. Us, Talking Heads, Patti Smith, we were miles and miles apart. I loved all the bands but I really loved The Ramones. They were so much fun and had such great songs. I knew them for a long time, since they were just starting and they're still one of my all-time favourites. There are people I miss too. Chris and I have often said it would have been wonderful to see what Johnny Thunders evolved into.

Letter to My Younger Self: Inspirational Women

I certainly have moments when it hits me I'm not young anymore. It was shocking and scary to age. So much of my notoriety was based on my looks. So to deal with that and try to look good... I've always tried, I think most women do. We survive on our looks. When I see current photographs I see my ageing process, that's where it shows up to me. But when I look in the mirror I see myself as I am and it's fine and I feel quite happy with the way I look.

Charlotte Rampling

Actor

12 November 2012

I was living in London at the beginning of the '60s when I was 16. I just wanted to be out there. I wanted to end school very quickly, which I did – I wasn't a good scholar. Then I did a secretarial course because my dad said I had to know how to earn my living. But I had a strong feeling that there was something out there for me and I was ready for things to happen. It was a good time to be young – lots of jobs about, you could take one job, leave it, try another job. It wasn't a stressful time, it was quite a utopian time – it didn't last long but I was right in the middle of it.

My parents were quite conventional parents for that time. My dad was a colonel in the army, my mother was a housewife. They were quite strict, quite straight, they were okay people. We didn't have a relationship at all like people do now. They were just 'the parents' – you didn't talk about feelings, just everyday things. You had the big conversations about life and ideals with your friends.

My feeling that things were going to happen to me was right. I was quite literally discovered in the street – King's Road, to be exact. My first job was as a temporary secretary in the typing pool at an advertising agency. I was 17. Someone noticed me – I was quite a good-looking girl – and asked me to come along and do a photograph for a Cadbury's advertisement. But the big one was when I was walking on the King's Road with my friend and someone asked me if I'd like to do a bit part in a film. It was Richard Lester's film *The Knack* – Lester of course made the Beatles' *A Hard Day's Night* and *Help!* They wanted lots of pretty girls for a scene. That was really the beginning of things for me. I thought straight away that being in a film was a fantastic way to make a living, much more fun than being a typist – but it was only on that level; this is fun. I had no ambition to be a great actress or anything, I just wanted to be out there 'in the groove' as we used to say.

I wouldn't want to tell my young self anything about making films. So much of it for me was about spontaneity, not knowing what was coming. I learned my life through living it. I educated myself. Though I have always thought it would have been great to have had a university life, I'd love to have done that. I love books and I love academia. I'd love to have been taught. But you can't have it both ways.

Most of my most important learning experiences have come through meeting people. Working with a director like Visconti, who has thought so much about life, what he does, what it means to do what he's doing. He was a lot older than me, I was a young actress when I worked with him. The

English actor Dirk Bogarde was one of the major pivots in my life. Those sort of people are like your masters. I hadn't really had any masters in the teaching world so they were very important to me, they were able to tell stories, give off the essence of their own lives so that I could understand things through them. I've always thought of being an actress as a way of being, a compliment to who you are. Each role is a part of you. I chose my roles very carefully, I had to have a relationship with them all.

When it comes to ageing, I do a lot of inside work, thinking work. I've always done that, it interests me. And I've come to certain conclusions which have helped me, a form of accepting. What can you do about it? You going to fight it? If you fight it, that's not going to change the fact that you're growing older. As an actress it's important to express yourself in each given decade. I decided to do that as me each time, not try to trick people or myself by changing my face. That's a form of trickery to me. I'm not against it, people can do it if they want to, but I have this quest for truth so I couldn't trick myself. What if I looked in the mirror and thought, oh shit, what the fuck have I done? That's not me!

I think the moments I've been in love have been the best moments in my life. It's a God-given gift when you fall in love. Nobody falls in love, more than twice or three times in their lives. Really falls in love, I mean. It's an incredible feeling. It doesn't necessarily last that long but it's so euphoric and all-encompassing. It can also be dangerous because you'd do anything. You're out of control, you're high on the most blissful drug in the world.

Sara Cox

Radio and TV presenter
9 April 2016

At 16, I was raving. I was the youngest of five and my eldest sister Dot really looked out for me. My mum didn't know I was cadging lifts with boys in their XR2s to drive me to go clubbing at Angels in Burnley. I had a real look going. My hair was a pineapple on the top of my head. I had a terrible spiral perm, my fringe held up with hairspray. I wore three pairs of knee socks and scrunched them down to my ankles so it looks like I had one of those massive tags you get when you're on probation. I'd have Kickers on, a Joe Bloggs t-shirt and huge parallel jeans that completely covered my feet. My best friend Joanne and I would drink Taboo and lemonade and have a grand old time.

During the week I was actually quite quiet and well behaved at school. I wasn't really a big fan of school. I remember people saying it was the best years of your life and I thought, God, I hope not, this is shit. I'd never been that happy at school – I'd been bullied because we'd moved around a couple of times. I was quite awkward, I got teased a lot. I got teased for having things like long skinny legs, big lips. Now I think, here I still am with long legs and big lips; that didn't turn out so badly.

I wouldn't go back to being a teenager, you don't have a Scooby-Doo about anything. I enjoyed getting older, getting more confident, learning what I wanted in life. I had a lot of male mates as an older teenager, I found them much less complicated than girls. I realise now I was just hanging out with the wrong kind of girls. Or maybe girls around the age of 16 are just a nightmare. But now I have lots of great female friends.

I was really lucky. I was living with my mum and stepdad and they worked really hard and a lot, but I had a very secure upbringing and I wasn't particularly angsty. I always had a feeling I'd be alright. I never really worried about getting a job, I think because I have my mum's work ethic and I've never been a snob about the kind of work I do. I'd worked since I was 14, behind a bar collecting glasses, on the door of a nightclub and then as a barmaid. I did have thoughts of becoming a vet but I knew I wouldn't stick with studying for all those years. Then I thought of joining the Mounted Police, because I was looking for a job where I could be sat on a saddle all day. I had vague thoughts of doing media at college but really, I didn't have a clue.

I always enjoyed writing and drama, and at home I'd play the fool and make people laugh. My grandad Vince was a real raconteur and joker. He went to comedy school for a couple of days; the dream was to get on *The Comedians*, that big TV show in the seventies. He never quite managed it. My sister told me tales of woe from college, having no shoes and living on a potato between 15 people and I thought, God, I don't fancy that much.

I got scouted as a model when I was in Paris, while I was walking around a clothes shop. They came up to me and said, 'You've got a really good look for now.' I think if that happened to my daughter now I'd just bustle her away. But I did that for a couple of years, and from that came the job presenting *The Girlie Show* (a magazine-format TV show in the '90s). So I thought, I'll do this presenting for a couple of years. Twenty years later, here I still am.

If I met the 16-year-old Sara now I don't think we'd have anything in common. She's 16! Maybe we'd go riding together, that's the only way we'd bond. She's a very different creature. I don't remember her very well. I still have little glimpses of self-doubt but nothing like I did at 16. It would blow her mind that I have three children. I didn't even look after my hamsters well, so looking after and feeding three small people would have been an outrageous thought. There are some things we'd have in common though. She tried to be a good person, and I've always done my best.

I don't have any career regrets, but I do think when I was presenting Breakfast on Radio 1, I was just knackered a lot of the time. I loved doing it but if you're really going to do that job you need to have a lot of early nights and I struggled with that because I'd be out every night. Part of the vibe of that show was us going out and doing what the audience was doing, being a bit wild. I guess if I hadn't done that, other parts of my career might have taken off sooner. Saying that, I was young. Then before I knew it, I had my first baby so that derailed me a bit. But to be truthful, I wouldn't change any of it.

I wasn't that ambitious or career-driven for the first ten years of working, I'm a lot more focused now. I think that's got a lot to do with my being with my husband Ben. I'm much more settled in my home life now, so I can focus on my career because I'm happier.

I think being a mum was always part of the plan. The marriage my first daughter came from didn't last for much more than a year after she was born (she split with DJ Jon Carter in 2005) but I don't have any regrets because the result was Lola. And she's a unique product of that marriage. More than any other kids who come afterwards, the first child is the real shaker. For the first time you can't put yourself first. It's also quite a nice excuse to take yourself off the merry-go-round. I absolutely loved being a mum. I've been asked to write parenting books but I kind of hate those. 'Oh look, you're a celebrity who's managed to have children, just like the billion women who came before you. Why wouldn't people want to read your children's cookbook?'

I said to Lola the other day, I don't know if I'm much good at this parenting lark and she said, 'Oh, Mum, you totally are, we're not too damaged.' I said, 'Oh, thanks, babe.' Everybody just muddles through, don't they?

Fearne Cotton

TV and radio presenter
7 October 2020

I had this really pivotal moment at 15 when I went from being a regular kid in school, who had a real passion for dance and drama, to being catapulted into the world of TV. Somebody at my local weekend drama club told me there were auditions for presenters on Disney. I went with very low expectations. There were a lot of kids from the big stage schools like the The BRIT School and Sylvia Young so I thought, I don't stand a chance here. But somehow I managed to get through. I really didn't feel like I knew what I was doing though. I was winging it. I just knew I wanted to be as successful as my TV heroes, people like Zoe Ball, Davina McCall, Chris Evans. I was loving every minute, but I didn't feel like 'I've found my place there and this is what I should be doing'. I felt like I'd woken up in a weird dream and I just walked into the telly. And there I suddenly was, interviewing Bewitched or the Spice Girls.

I can still vividly picture the moment I found out I had the job at Disney. There were three people up for the last audition, which was an on-air interview with Andi Peters. Later, on TV they announced who'd got the job. So I was just watching with my family, all sat in the front room in my house in the suburbs in Eastcote in Northwest London. And I was thinking, I'm really crapping myself here but I doubt it's going to be me, so let's not get too excited. So when they said my name out loud, me, my mum, dad and brother, we just went bonkers. We were jumping about, screaming. It was like something out of a film. Here I was, just a regular kid going about my life, with a deep desire and passion to work in this industry. Then all of a sudden, out of the blue, this moment happens. It was really special. I don't think I've ever had a work high like it since. That first yes or foot in the door is the best, it really is. And I'm still trying to keep my foot in the door now, quite frankly.

My only real preoccupation at the time was work. I didn't want to do anything else. I didn't go out and drink in the park with my mates, I missed my school prom, I didn't go to many birthday parties, because I was so focused on not cocking up this amazing experience and opportunity. I'm a bit of a nerd anyway, I've always been studious when it comes to the things I love. So I would go to bed really early and make sure I'd had enough sleep and learnt all my lines. And I was also trying to do my GCSEs at the same time, which was not ideal.

From the start I definitely had this anxiety that I didn't belong. I remember so clearly standing in the studio looking around thinking, how are they so accomplished, how are these pop bands taking up that space and feeling really solid about it? I feel like I'm still the suburban school girl and I felt that until I got into my 30s. It's really only since I started doing Happy Place (her interview podcast focusing on mental health) that I really felt I could occupy this space confidently. Later, I realised that lots of people feel like that. So many of us go along, silently worrying we don't fit in, and not saying it out loud. Actually, there's a real liberation in just saying it and having this person who you assume is incredibly confident saying they feel the same. You realise we're all in the same boat. It's really lovely knowing that.

It makes me feel a bit sad thinking back to the naively optimistic 16-year-old I was. As a young kid, all through my teens and most of my 20s, I had this really beautiful soft naivety that I've definitely lost now. It really allowed me to see the best in people, and to believe that anything was possible, and to dream really big. That really helped me keep moving forward in my career for a long time because I wasn't willing to accept the word no or to give up. I always felt like I could try again.

I did have a couple of things change in me as I went into my thirties. Firstly, women's hormones change dramatically round about 35. There's a huge sudden descent which can result in depression or anxiety. And for me specifically, there were lots of things in my late 20s, early 30s that I felt really not okay about. I dropped into this depression for a couple of years and I had to sort of start from scratch again. It was quite a drastic disenchantment. I didn't believe in all the dreams I had previously held. I didn't believe in the myths of what the job or the industry meant. I didn't believe in the grandeur of it. I didn't believe in having this insane fear-based respect for everybody in it. I just dropped all of that and wanted to start again. And that was terrifying, but it's been essential in me ending up where I am now, doing a job I care deeply about.

I had a bit of an emotional collapse when I was going through that time of being constantly papped by the newspapers. It was really intense in my 20s. I had a very unhealthy relationship with the press. You feel misrepresented and misunderstood, which is a really horrible feeling. And you lose your sense of who you are. You're so busy trying to be what everybody else wants you to be, and to avoid being attacked. So you do your best to remain small and quiet yet live a life, and you actually forget who you are. Now I don't care, people can say what they want. I've been to hell and back, so now it's about being me and if people don't like that, it's really none of my business. My business is to do what makes me tick. I don't go anywhere exciting or glamorous. I'm a homebody. I build my life around my house and my family and that's what makes me feel really happy. That's the only way to stay sane.

Luckily, having children gave me such perspective it was the healthiest thing that could have happened to me. I could just focus on what I gave a shit about. It's obviously exhausting and can be really hard to navigate in the modern world, but I was really lucky in that I gained two stepchildren before I became a mother. So I had this really nice tester period of sharing my time with four people, and feeling like an extra layer of support. I have a beautiful relationship with my stepkids and I feel very lucky every day about that. Family life has cemented me in the arena that I really care about – family connection, love, support. It was all there before but life was so busy and hectic that those ties became weaker and weaker. Travelling around the world so often, I wouldn't get to see my actual family that much. As soon as I had stepkids and then my own kids that all just stopped and I said no, I'm not going anywhere.

Letter to My Younger Self: Inspirational Women

If I could travel back to any moment in my life it would be when I was on holiday in Mexico with my best mate Lolly, about ten years ago. We'd both had a bit of a rocky time – I'd just come out of a failed engagement. She was in the shower, and I was sat outside our lovely little hut near the beach with a beer, just looking at the sky on this beautiful sunny balmy evening. And I just had this moment of unexpected euphoria. There was no particular reason to feel happy; obviously I was in a lovely location but there wasn't anything on my horizon to look forward to, there wasn't anything in the past that I was especially happy about. It was just cinematic. I've thought about that moment so many times because it was so perfect and gorgeous, but it wasn't connected to anything happening in my life. It was just this very powerful euphoria for no reason. I've never forgotten about it and I often daydream back to that moment, and I would love to relive it.

Chapter 13:

Hindsight

Kathy Burke

Actor, writer and director

4 June 2012

When I look back to being a teenager the thing I remember most is the food. I remember the first time I had Chinese spare ribs, and the first time I had eggy bread. At home I was a moody miserable thing who didn't want to clean her room, but with my friends I was a pretty happy person. I loved my friends and my music, especially punk and two tone. Youth is wasted on the young though. I do think, my God, if only I'd known then what I know now. Youth is so beautiful and so special. It doesn't matter how fat you are, or if you have wonky teeth – youth is just beautiful.

I did worry that boys didn't fancy me – the ones round our flats just thought I was fat and ugly. And I worried about the fashion then, boob tubes and satin trousers. I thought, oh God, my bum's too fat for those trousers. And have I actually got boobs? But that was the joy of punk coming along. It was such a relief. I could just wear jeans and flat caps and be a tomboy. It was a way of hiding my physicality and I felt real security in that. I remember when I first saw (punk icon) Poly Styrene on *Top of the Pops*, in her braces and twin-set suit. She was like an angel, the coolest thing I'd ever seen.

I was told by teachers at school I couldn't be an actress 'cause of the way I talked and how I looked. But when I got into the Anna Scher theatre club, she thought it was the best idea I'd ever had in my life and everything would be fine. I was very lucky to have an inspirational woman like that in my life at such a young age. And I met all these extraordinary people at the theatre. Suddenly all the boys wanted to talk to me. They didn't fancy me, but they thought I was a laugh, they liked me.

I'd tell my younger self not to drink so much. I'd say, don't think you need to get pissed to be funny, to have a personality. My life only started to get complicated and upsetting when booze got involved. Before that I was able to just bob along and enjoy life. But drink is a very powerful thing. It fucked up my early twenties on a personal level. I misjudged things, blokes mainly. I grew up in a house where Dad had a massive drink problem yet the moment I was able to have a drink I did. It's amazing really. It made me forget about everything, I could suddenly just be happy. Maybe I could get where Dad was coming from. Luckily, it did dawn on me and in my mid-twenties I stopped completely for three years. But I wish I'd done it sooner. Because I didn't really know who I was.

You never go into a job expecting it to be a hit. When I first worked with Harry Enfield doing The Slobs (the comedy characters she and Enfield played) I didn't really get them, I thought they were a bit patronising. Then when we put the costumes on, I got it; they were cartoons with catchphrases, it was harmless. But when we came to do another series I went to Paul Whitehouse (who also created and played characters on Harry Enfield's sketch show) and said, 'Look, I think I've got more to give – playing this fat, smoking woman, it's not really a stretch.' And he had the idea of putting Kevin the teenager with a character I'd created, Perry the pubescent. I loved Perry, the little fella.

I fell out of love with acting a few years ago. I think the real reason is that I was suffering with a very bad stomach condition that had been going on for years without my knowing it. I started to lose energy for acting. I don't want to sound like a wanker but when you act it should come from the core, like an opera singer. You have to feel the character from the inside. And I couldn't feel anything anymore. I was doing it all from my head and it didn't feel right. I used to get a real buzz out of acting so not to have that buzz any more was so deflating, I asked myself why I was doing it. I didn't want to do it because I was in a comfortable position career-wise. But I loved writing about the buzz I had as a girl (in the semi-autobiographical TV series *Walking and Talking*) because I was writing for a brilliant young actress who has it all in front of her, and I loved that.

Lorraine Kelly

Journalist and TV presenter
4 September 2008

At 16, I was rather shy and what would be called a 'late developer'. I was just about to meet my first serious boyfriend. I liked school but I was also a bit of a rebel. I used to wear a circle on my head like David Bowie and I painted my 'Jesus' sandals with silver sparkly nail polish. I also embroidered 'Bowie' on the back and on the pockets of my blue duffel coat with pink thread.

If I could go back, I'd shout at my young self, 'You have a fabulous figure, wear a bikini and have a bit more confidence.' I worried about my weight but despite being shy, I was always good at talking to people and could fill awkward silences.

I would tell my teenage self that if you work hard enough and if you are straight and honest then you will get there in the end. I was supposed to go to university but when a job at the local paper, the *East Kilbride News*, came up, I went for it. I don't have any regrets other than not having a social life for all the time I worked as a reporter – but that was the price I paid for landing such a fantastic job.

I'd tell my 16-year-old self NOT to have that party! My mum and dad were on holiday and the house got wrecked. That is something I am still very ashamed of and I would like to go back and tell myself not to be so selfish. I would also tell myself not to be so mean to my little brother, who was six years younger than me and a lovely wee boy. We fought like cat and dog, mainly because I felt very usurped by him when he was born. It didn't help that he was the cutest baby anyone had ever seen. We get on really well now, but I wish I had been kinder to him.

I would tell my younger self not to worry about silly little things, but to enjoy life more and maybe not be such a little workhorse. And I'd tell her the best is still to come – you will meet an adorable man who will want to marry you, be lucky enough to have a daughter and to land one of the best jobs in TV.

Gabby Logan

Sports presenter and former gymnast
1 February 2016

When I was 16, I was completely focused on gymnastics, training and competing. It absorbed my life. I got the bit between my teeth when I was about ten, and I decided I wanted to be really good (she represented Wales at the 1990 Commonwealth Games). I was quite focused as a young girl.

Sport is so good for your hormones. I think it helped me get through puberty more easily than I might have otherwise. It's quite a powerful thing to know your body is capable of so many things, and gymnastics keeps you in tune with your body. So that's useful when your body starts changing, to know that your body is about more than just how it looks, to know it can be a very powerful thing.

Just before I went to university my brother Daniel died. He was 15. That was a massive change in my life, in my whole outlook. It was a life-changing thing for all of us. It blew the family apart. My parents were divorced within 10 years.

My dad (Leeds/Wales footballer Terry Yorath) had a lot of problems. It unraveled us all and we had to work our way back together. If I'd ever wavered about going to university, I was right back on track. I wanted to achieve something. I almost felt like I was living two lives. My brother had just signed for Leeds United. He was 15, and he'd already been asked to play for Wales' under-18s. He was really talented and a natural leader, very popular, obvious captain material. He was never going to pursue his dreams now, so I didn't want to waste any opportunity to pursue mine. I arrived at university with a very mature approach to life because of what I'd gone through. I wanted to join every society, try every sport, get whatever I could out of it.

I studied law with a vague idea I might be a barrister. But I missed sport massively and I was trying to find a new way to do it. I'd go swimming and think, am I good enough to be a swimmer? Could I be a runner? When I was a gymnast I'd become exposed to media and TV and I was aware of it through my dad. I got some media work during my gap year, on a local radio station, and while I was at university I kept working there, reading the news at weekends. Then the Monday after I graduated I started on the Breakfast Show.

My 16-year-old self would have been absolutely beside herself to think I'd be going to rugby World Cups, football World Cups, and most of all doing the Olympics show on the BBC that I did in 2012. I used to sit and watch Trans World Sport on a Saturday morning and there was a female who did the voiceover – I never even saw her face – but I was so impressed by her, whoever she was. I thought she was amazing. I thought gosh, I'd love to do that. I do get letters from girls saying they want to be female broadcasters but I hope that changes and they start just saying they want to be broadcasters.

I don't think we should expect all of our sports stars to have the personality of Michael McIntyre, but there's a long time after you've finished playing your sport that you need to be a human being, so it's good to practise. And people don't forget. It often happens in our industry that you come across someone and you just think, they'll make a great pundit one day. I met Tom Daley when he was just 13 and immediately I thought he was adorable. Brilliant person, fantastic to be around. I met Andy Murray early in his career and really enjoyed spending the day with him too. I knew he would win things and be a big star. But of course you meet other people too, the kind who just burn their bridges.

It was all very quick when I met my husband (Scottish rugby player Kenny Logan). I think we both felt very early on in our relationship that we were going to be together for a long time. I have vivid memories of our meeting – it was 17 years ago last Saturday. We were discussing that night just last week and we can both remember it very clearly. My kids are always asking me about how we met so we've talked about it a lot. As for being a mum, I don't think I even thought about it, it's just something I wanted to do ever since I was a kid. I always imagined myself as a mum.

Growing up with quite a famous dad, I always knew it wasn't the be-all and end-all. I never wanted to be famous, I just wanted to have a really interesting job. Being in the media can be awkward but it's not a major problem for me. As you get older, you learn how to put things into perspective, and you probably learn to be more guarded. I was misquoted in a story about Andy Murray. I was doing a Q&A for students about broadcasting, and I was asked a question about great interviews I'd done. I said how much I'd enjoyed spending time with him, but the next time I met him he'd lost and he was a bit grumpy, which he had every right to be. The point was, just because you've had a good time with someone once, it doesn't mean the next time you interview them they're your best friend. But of course, *The Mail* decided to take it a different way. But that's nature of some journalism these days.

I wouldn't actually want to relive giving birth to my twins, but I loved those first few weeks of having my babies home from hospital. When I actually gave birth I had a massive haemorrhage and lost half the blood in my body so I had to stay in hospital for a bit longer. I actually got a bit institutionalised. I was a bit nervous about how I'd adapt to the outside world. But I remember arriving home and the dogs coming to meet the babies in the drive, then we all went into the house together and started life as a family. Within about an hour it felt great. Kenny was amazing. He'd just given up professional rugby so he was able to take it slowly, and we were able to really enjoy that time with them. It was really, really special. But honestly, I still feel like that now. I love waking them up in the morning. And I love going in at night, when they're asleep and they look so cuddle-able, and giving their sweaty brows a kiss.

Dame Jacqueline Wilson

Author

21 February 2008

I was painfully shy at 16, but I had a bit of initiative too. I knew very much I wanted to be a writer and at 17 years old, I left Kingston and went up to Dundee to work for the publisher D.C. Thomson as a trainee journalist, which seems quite brave now. Looking back, I see those two years as the most vivid of my life.

Life was very different when you were 16 in the '60s. I loved to go dancing and sometimes went up to London to dancehalls by myself, which sounds incredible now. I didn't feel cool but I tried to act it. I was just starting to earn enough money to buy my own clothes – I adored my dolly rocker, quite a cheap but very stylish '60s dress. I loved the Beatles and I went to see the Rolling Stones and Gerry &

The Pacemakers at the Caird Hall in Dundee. It was a great time to be young.

I wish I'd known then how to put boyfriends into perspective. At 16, I broke up with a boy after 18 months and I thought it was absolutely the worst thing that could ever have happened to me. You feel like you're in love and it's the most wonderful thing ever and no one can understand you. But the one thing experience shows you is that the person you're passionately in love with at 16 is not the person you're in love with at 60. Looking back now, that boy and I had nothing in common at all.

I'd like to tell the teenage me not to be in such a hurry. I was mad enough to get married at 19 and I remember my grandmother saying I should wait until I was 25. I thought she was completely crazy. I didn't realise how difficult it would be to live with someone else, how many petty rows you can have. By the time I was 21, I had a baby. I adore my daughter but it seems so sad that at 21, when you really should be having a whale of a time, that I was hauling bags of sugar and potatoes about and changing nappies.

Chapter 14:

Love

Alison Steadman

Actor

1 September 2014

At 16, I was already doing youth theatre and loving it. I wanted to be an actress but I was too young to leave home and go to drama school in London. I was already aware of the wrench it was going to be when I left my family and Liverpool, the city I loved, but in the early sixties it seemed the only way to become an actress. I also went to college to learn shorthand and book-keeping – my dad said if I wanted to become an actress I should have something to fall back on when I didn't have work. But they loved getting me to entertain the family with impersonations.

My mum didn't want me to leave home but she told me I had a real talent, and when I did go to drama school my parents were thrilled that I was venturing out, rather than settling down with a couple of babies, or working in a shop. The day I left, my dad said I was going to have the most wonderful amazing adventure which would inform the rest of my life, even if the acting didn't work out. And if it didn't, he said, never be afraid to come home and say you tried. I'm sad they weren't around to see me get my OBE, and that my dad didn't see me doing *The Rise and Fall of Little Voice* onstage or getting my Olivier Award. But they both saw *Abigail's Party* and loved it.

I loved living in Liverpool in the sixties – with bands like the Beatles, Gerry & The Pacemakers. We were all mad on going to The Cavern nightclub. I had to sneak there because my mum didn't want me going to this underground den where pop groups played. But it was wonderful, and I met John and Paul there when I was 16. I was thrilled to bits. They weren't famous yet – they hadn't made a record – they were on the cusp of all that. I liked Paul better – he was friendly, and John was a bit scary.

My mum and dad had a great marriage, they were lovely. I called my mum the wise old owl, she was one of those people who was pretty sharp and I feel she was one of those people who probably regretted that she hadn't had a career. Sometimes she would say to me, 'I wish I'd had a better education.' She was quite sad about that, a potential that was never tapped. I think a lot of people feel like that. My dad could play the violin and he loved art – when he retired, he started to paint. He was really good. It's such a shame he couldn't go to art school but he had to go to work when he was 15.

I had a lovely boyfriend when I was 17. If I could back and meet up with anyone from my past it would be Jimmy. He was such a great, gentle guy and we got on so well. We used to sing together – he had a voice like Frank Sinatra. But when I got to 18, I became very nervous about staying in the same place with the same person. So, even though I loved him, I finished with him. I remember we sobbed in each other's arms when we said goodbye. He said, 'If you change your mind, let me know.' I never saw him again. In different circumstances, at a different time, we could have stayed together for the rest of our lives.

If I was trying to impress the teenage Alison, I'd show her *Abigail's Party*. That character was devised by me and (her then husband) Mike Leigh. We started with a blank sheet of paper and we improvised and we ended up with *Abigail*. I feel very proud of that. I was four months pregnant when we filmed it for TV. Thirty-six years later, people still stop me in the street to talk about it.

I'm still generally the positive person I was when I was younger but lately something has happened with me. I do now have what I call dark days when I get very down. It has nothing to do with happiness in my life, because I am happy, but I think I'm looking back more than looking forward. All my aunts and uncles have gone, my mum and dad have gone. It's life, we can't live forever. But sometimes a depression does come over me, which I have to fight to shake off. I have to count all the pluses in my life. It's weird. I never thought I'd be like this.

Recently I had a wobbly time when I thought I couldn't go back on stage. I was in my late sixties and I thought I'd peaked. It takes courage to be an actress and suddenly it felt too scary. But I'm on stage now and I'd give myself a pat on the back for that. I took a deep breath and jumped. So often I've worried that I was about to be found out for being rubbish. I've been scared so many times in my acting life, but I've ended up doing it anyway.

I'm going to sound sentimental but I'd love to go back in time to when I gave birth to my two sons. Just to look at them so young. I remember when they were born, looking at them and thinking, my God, I just made that child! They were the two best days of my life. And then when they smile for the first time. I remember my mum telling me how my dad was holding me when I smiled for the first time and he was so thrilled. And I remember my husband holding my son, talking to him and he suddenly looked up at me and said, 'He smiled at me!' When that happens – ah! It's like the world just glows a brighter colour.

Dame Jane Goodall

Primatologist and anthropologist

20 September 2012

I was an extremely happy teenager, having grown up in a very close family. Life was wonderful, even though we were all just recovering from the war and no one had any money. I was a shy child, but I loved to have fun and I was very determined. I think I was better at things than I thought I was. My mother made sure I read and read and read. I'd love to find a young person to work with now who is like I was then – I had such a passion.

I became obsessed with the idea of going to Africa when I was a very young girl. I read the Tarzan books and of course I fell completely in love with Tarzan. I felt he'd married the wrong Jane – it should have been me. I was very jealous of Jane. My mum saved up to take me to see a Tarzan film at the cinema but a few minutes in, I got very upset and had to be taken out. I said, 'That wasn't Tarzan.' Johnny Weissmuller was not how I imagined Tarzan at all. And to this day I've never watched another Tarzan film.

I knew I wanted to go to Africa and be with animals, but I wasn't thinking about it from a career point of view at all. I wasn't thinking of primates either – they were too esoteric to really enter my thinking. I was just dreaming of the jungle, and the wild open plains. In those days girls were all supposed to wait for the white knight to come along and sweep us up in matrimony and we wouldn't have to worry about a career. When I told people what I wanted to do everyone laughed. 'Where would I get the money to do that?', they said – and anyway, I was a girl! But my mother was amazing. She just said, 'If you really want something worthwhile, never give up.'

It wasn't reading books or working with chimps which convinced me animals could think and feel. It was my dog Rusty. We spent every waking hour together. Every day started with him barking outside the door at 6am to be let in, and from that moment we were glued together all day. I can still remember clearly the day he died. I was about 20 and in London out to dinner with my boyfriend and I got a call. I was told the news and I went back to the table and tried to carry on but my boyfriend looked at me and said, 'Something's wrong, isn't it?' And I burst out crying. I was utterly devastated. His dying changed things for me – I could never have left England when he was still alive. The deaths of some of the chimps I've worked with were very upsetting but it wasn't the same as Rusty. The chimps were their own selves, they were quite separate – Rusty was part of me.

When I finally got there, Africa was everything I'd dreamt

it would be. I had a wild time on the boat going over – flirted outrageously – then I went up on the train from Mombasa through Kenya. I was picked up at the station and we drove off in the dark and I saw an aardvark, and a giraffe. In those days it was still wild, untouched Africa. There were no roads, no trails – just us and lions and rhinos and African wildlife. I couldn't believe it was happening to me, it was magic, magic, magic.

If I had been told back then the kind of life I'm living now, I would have given up. The idea of speaking to audiences would have utterly terrified me. That wasn't the life I wanted to live. When I began my work studying primates, I knew I was different to everyone else in the field. I was female, and I didn't have a degree and I had my own ideas about animals. When Louis (Leakey, Kenyan archaeologist who raised funds for Goodall's chimpanzee research at Cambridge University) got me in to do my PhD, they told me I'd done everything wrong. They told me only humans had emotions. I was utterly shocked – but I remembered Rusty and I knew they were wrong.

Judith Kerr

Author and illustrator

22 May 2017

We came to London when I was a teenager, three years before the war. The Second World War broke out a few weeks after my 16th birthday. On my 17th birthday the Germans marched into Paris, and then came the Blitz in London. We learned English quickly and at that point, my brother and I still felt we were having an adventure. We felt we'd had a very good childhood, much better than if there had been no Hitler and we'd just stayed in Germany. It was so interesting. We went to Switzerland, then Paris, then London. If you arrive in a country and can't understand what anyone is staying, then a year later you are speaking their language, that gives you a tremendous boost. It's a huge credit to my parents that we felt that way. They were always very positive in front of us.

My main preoccupation at that point was a conviction that I wouldn't live to be 18. Everyone expected the invasion of Britain and we knew my father (Alfred Kerr, a prominent

German-Jewish arts critic) was on a Nazi blacklist. They'd put a price on his head. We all felt if the Nazis got into Britain that would be it for us.

The Blitz was pretty tough. We lived in Bloomsbury, which got it bad because the enemy planes went for the stations, but we never experienced any hostility as German refugees. People were most generous, extraordinarily so. No one ever said anything nasty to us. There were three types of alien: enemy aliens who were the Germans and Italians; friendly: aliens, like the French and Poles; and people like my family, who were German but known to be very anti-Hitler. We were friendly enemy aliens.

All the way through the war, I was always drawing. Eventually the Blitz quietened down, and I started going to evening art classes. I began to realise that this was what I wanted to do. It was a great help. It gave me something to live for. I was very shy. And always worrying dreadfully what people thought of me, and whether I had said or done the wrong thing. If I could talk to that teenage girl now, I'd tell her to hang on in there, it's going to be alright. And don't worry so much what other people think about you. Though that would be empty advice because I still worry now.

My husband was a very keen photographer and we would look through pictures he'd taken of our lives together – we were married for 52 years. The children said how nice I looked when I was young and I thought I looked nice too. I wish I'd known then. I didn't think I was good-looking. I spent the whole time thinking, oh dear, this isn't right.

My husband (scriptwriter Nigel Kneale) changed my life. He was a writer, he wrote the *Quatermass* serials (a TV drama series broadcast in the 1950s). When I met him, he was working for the BBC, just doing any old job, writing for children's shows, adapting plays for television. He taught me a lot about writing and encouraged me all the time. I struggled when I tried to write *When Hitler Stole Pink Rabbit*, the book about my childhood. I found it so hard to do. I said to him, 'This is no good. I can't do it.' He read what I'd written, which was a terrible mess, in pen and pencil, with things scrubbed out and scribbled in, and he said, 'No, this is good. You must finish it.' But you can't just write about moving around all those countries. Hitler has to be on the first page. In the end, I got him on the second page.

It was very exciting when they published *The Tiger Who Came to Tea*. Even more so when it was a success, but I had no idea it would pass through the generations the way it has. It was the first thing I ever did, just a bedtime story I made up for my daughter. I saw her little face, wanting to be entertained, so I just put in everything she liked. We'd seen tigers in the zoo but we didn't talk about how dangerous they were. We just thought they were incredibly beautiful, with that incredible deep orange. My daughter wanted to stroke them. So the thought of one coming to your house – wouldn't that be lovely? And she was crazy about the idea of going to a café unexpectedly, at night, in the dark, so I put that in too. People have looked for metaphors but no, it was a real tiger.

The teenage me would be in total, total amazement if you told her about her success in the future. All I ever hoped for then was some way of being able to pay the rent while being a painter. I thought maybe I could get a job as a ticket clippie on a bus and get a very early shift so that I could paint for the rest of the time.

I was very close to my father, who died in 1948, and I still have conversations in my head with him. Someone has just written a new biography of him and there was a lot that was new to me. I didn't know just how bad it was for my parents. There's a letter in that book in which my father says, 'Fortunately, the children haven't realised what the real situation is.' We just knew they didn't have much money. We didn't know they were terrified for their lives. My father was so loathed by the Nazis. When they came to power, no one was allowed to pay him any money. Suddenly we had nothing. All our belongings were confiscated. We moved to Switzerland because he hoped to write for a big Swiss newspaper he'd written for before, but they were very worried about antagonising the Germans so they refused to have anything to do with him. I didn't know any of this. But it did make me feel proud when I understood.

If I could go back and relive any time it would be when my husband and I were first married. We'd finally got a tiny council flat just behind Kensington Church Street – it was difficult to find anywhere in the fifties because everywhere had been bombed and they were in the process of re-building. I remember going out for a walk in Kensington Gardens one Sunday and suddenly just realising, this wasn't a special occasion. We're completely free to do this any Sunday we want. And it was wonderful.

Jackie Kay

Poet, playwright and novelist
13 March 2008

I'd be happy to be the 16-year-old Jackie Kay's best friend. I liked a good laugh, I was good company. And I was kind – I blow-dried my mum's hair and I sent her a letter every day when she was in hospital. I was quite an unusual teenager – I had a mum who was quite ill a lot of the time so I was looking after her rather than the other way around. That makes you grow up quite fast.

I'd tell myself not to worry about being gay. At 16, I was already in love with a girl but I wasn't out yet and I did worry about it, whether it was abnormal, and whether my family would accept it. I'd tell my old self not to bother looking over her shoulder and instead to embrace everything about who she is and be proud of it.

I'd tell my 16-year-old-self to have more faith and confidence in her writing. I started writing at age 12 but I didn't think I'd be a writer. I thought I'd be an actress. I would tell her to know that she will make mistakes and end up hating about 80 per cent of what she writes but that's part of being a real writer.

I think the secret of happiness is not to bother about money or weight. I'd tell my old self to try to help other people and not bother with material things at all. I'd warn her that in another 30 years society will be even more obsessed with obesity and weight and she must learn to be happy with her body.

The most important thing I'd tell her is not to smoke – or she'll still be smoking 30 years later. And I'd tell her to stop drinking Blue Nun and not to spend so much time talking on the phone – her parents have to pay for it!

I'd tell my old self that in the course of her life she'll have a series of big loves and she shouldn't get hung up on any of them. The world is a big place and there are lots of loves out there and in the course of your life you'll find some of them. I'd tell her that a broken heart mends just like a broken leg does, that time changes the way you see everything. And she'd be surprised when I told her her biggest love would be her son and it would be parting with him when he went to university that would hurt the most.

Kay Mellor

Actor, writer and director
9 February 2021

When I was 16 my main preoccupation was being pregnant. I was about to have my first child, with nowhere to live and no income. I'd left school and gone to secretarial college. Back then, you could either be a secretary, a nurse, or a teacher if you were a woman. Those were three things that were open to you. As I was a bit of a writer and wanted to do drama, my mum said, if you do a secretarial course for a year, you can go to drama school. So that was the deal. Then when I was at secretarial college, I got pregnant.

When I first found out I was pregnant it was a catastrophe. Anthony was my first proper boyfriend. We'd been going out for about 18 months. We had no money. He was very optimistic, ecstatic that I was pregnant and having a child. But I remember feeling, this is terrible, this is the end of my life. My mother was horrified. And when she came around to the idea, she said look, you don't have to marry him if you don't want. You can stay here and have the baby. And for that I'm eternally grateful to her, because there's not many mothers who would have said that. In those days if you were pregnant you got married, and very hastily. I wasn't forced to marry. But actually, I did love Anthony. And he loved me. We saw each other every single day for 18 months. We were obsessed with each other. So we did get married. Somebody made a dress for me, somebody organised a special licence, and this wedding, which I had nothing to do with organising, went ahead, with everybody crying all through it. The vicar wouldn't marry us in the church. Anthony wanted to have a church wedding, but the vicar said no, it won't last two minutes.

Everybody I knew on our estate had a mum and dad, apart from me. I just had a mum. People used to say to me, to tease me, you haven't got a dad. But I remembered the breakup, it was a very violent breakup. Those images don't go away, ever, ever, ever, ever. You will remember them all your life. When my dad came back into my life when I was 21, I found it very difficult to make a relationship with him. But I didn't need two parents; my mother was a mother and a father to us. She was a very affectionate, loving woman who, if she wasn't working, was making sure that me and my brother were alright and given love. She was a brilliant mother, she made me believe I could do anything. I had a wonderful childhood in many ways, because having one loving parent is all you really need.

Growing up, I didn't know anybody that was a writer or an actress. I had no thoughts of going to drama school, I didn't know what that was. Then one day I was entertaining the class during dinner break – making up little sketches and stories as I often did – and Mrs Davis, an American teacher, came into the classroom. I didn't even know she was there, I was so wrapped up in acting out. After all the kids finished clapping, she sent everyone out and asked me to stay behind. I thought I was going to get into trouble. And she said, 'How do you do that? Where does the story come from? Is it written down?' And I told her I just make it up on the spot. And she said, 'I wish I could put you in my pocket and take you back to the States with me.'

I had no idea what she was talking about, but after that day, I was chosen to go to everything in school that was art, even a trip to the ballet. It was always me and I never understood why. And when my mother went to the open day, Mrs Davis said, she needs to go to drama school. She's got a talent. My mum was kind of furious, saying, you've got your head in the clouds, Kay, you need to concentrate on your maths and sciences. But slowly she came round to the idea and realised that what Mrs Davis was saying was true.

They say that, even when you're 30, you're a young writer, because you need life experience to be able to write. I had a lot of life experience at a young age. And that meant I was never fearful. When you've given birth at 16, when you don't know where your next penny is coming from, you're not afraid of saying things. I remember the producer of *Band of Gold* (the 1995 TV series created by Mellor) telling me what he thought my series was, saying it should be this and that. And I said to him, no, it's none of those things. It's about the women that walk the streets in Bradford, it's about prostitution, it's about sex workers. I said, you should get your hat and coat on and go up to Bradford and meet those women, like I did. And then you wouldn't tell me what my series is really about. It takes a certain courage to talk to a producer like that. I think my life experience, so different to his, gave me that courage.

Kay Mellor

Anthony and I did go through a bit of a rough patch. When I went into further education, Bretton Hall College, Anthony was out earning a living, looking after the kids and putting a roof over our heads. And I was moving in a different direction, towards drama, writing, acting. In many ways, I was leaving him behind. He was stuck in that alpha male, motor mechanic, 'got to put the food on the table, got to pay the mortgage', breadwinner mindset. I mention Willy Russell – *Educating Rita*, that was my story. I should have written that. I always felt like he beat me to it.

But God bless Anthony, he knew that if we were to sustain our marriage, he would have to change. So he went to Stockport College and got a degree in social welfare. And he became interested in education and politics. There was one day, we'd gone on holiday, maybe to Majorca, with the kids. And we were sat on that beach, and we were like talking about things that interested both of us. Our minds were both opening. We were still juggling two small girls, and we had bills to pay, but we were connecting on a different level to how we had as young people. We were looking at architecture, noticing things. Our brains were both starting to open. And I started to grow closer to him.

I think if the 16-year-old Kay could look at me now and see that people actually know my name, and see that I make television, and that my name goes up as writer and creator and director... I think that would blow her brains out. In a million years, she could never have dreamt that. And she'd also see that you can be happy in a long relationship if you work at it. I've said so many times, people fall in and out of love. And that's alright. Look for what it was that fundamentally attracted you to that person. Not just the physicality, but that

317

person underneath, the letter in the envelope. Don't throw it away, because you'll just have another letter. And then you'll get bored of reading that letter.

If I could go back and live one day from my past again, it would be from the first time I went to the Caribbean. It was a mind-blowing moment because it was such a different culture. We'd never seen anything like it. It was our first big holiday and Anthony's 40th birthday. We went to Barbados, St Lucia. It was just like paradise. It took my breath away, it was so utterly beautiful. A sort of simple life, but so beautiful. I remember standing on our hotel balcony, watching the fish being netted by these young Caribbean lads. The sun, the sunsets, the palm trees, the colour of the sea, the colour of the little houses – everything about it was glorious. I felt like I was in a great big film. Those images will stay with me all my life.

The Big Issue was launched in 1991 by John Bird and Gordon Roddick. The aim was clear and simple: to offer the poorest in society – those who are homeless or at risk of homelessness, the marginalised and the dispossessed – an opportunity to earn a legitimate income. They would work to build their own futures. It was a hand up, not a handout.

The means to this future was a campaigning, challenging, compassionate magazine that would be produced by *The Big Issue* team then bought for half the cover price by those in need for them to sell on the street. The difference between the two sums was the income people made.

This identity and means of working has remained hardwired at our core for over 30 years. The magazine, produced by a team of professional journalists, retains an outsider agenda. We give those ignored or without platform in the regular media a voice. We don't speak for those left behind, we invite them to speak for themselves. Then we challenge those in power to do something about it.

Content is key. It is funny, not fusty, pointed, informed, able to access the biggest names and have them reveal things they simply won't to others. Those people, like readers, trust *The Big Issue*. We now have a rapidly expanding online offering. Today, bigissue.com continues to grow as a world-leading site for news around social change.

The act of selling on the street was revolutionary. Growing out from London, over 210 million copies of *The Big Issue* have been sold in Britain. It has enabled vendors to earn over £115million, money that otherwise would have come from illegal means or handouts. Over 92,000 men and women have worked their way out of poverty selling *The Big Issue*.

Big Issue has inspired a global network. There are now over 100 similar street magazines across the world, including *Big Issues* in Australia, Japan, South Korea, Taiwan and South Africa. *The Big Issue* in Britain now also has a successful social investment arm called Big Issue Invest as well as a shop.

Today, Big Issue Group brings together our media, investment and service initiatives under a shared mission to create innovative solutions through enterprise, to unlock social and economic opportunity for the 14.5 million people in the UK living in poverty to earn, learn and thrive.

The Big Issue challenges that which is not right. We stand up for what is.

Paul McNamee
UK Editor, *The Big Issue*